The Resurrection - Ruse or Reality?

The Resurrection on Trial

L. James Harvey, PhD

L. James Harvey, PhD

CROSSLINK
PUBLISHING

The Resurrection - Ruse or Reality?

P CrossLink Publishing
C www.crosslink.org

ISBN 978-0-9826215-6-1

To my loving wife, Jackie, mother of our four wonderful children Linda, Douglas, Leslie, and Lisa and my partner and friend for 58 years. She served as the initial editor, and provided the love and encouragement without which this work could not have come to full fruition

Reviews and Endorsements

The minute I began reading I was drawn into story of what several first century AD witnesses might say if they were placed on the witness stand in a modern courtroom. The responses of Peter, Caiaphas, Pilate, and Mary Magdalene are intriguing, sometimes just what you would expect them to say, sometimes not. Throughout, the text moves quickly- the legal questions and responses are always brief, the text never complicated or stuffy. I think this volume will be fascinating reading for many, as it draws the reader through several relevant issues and on to the ultimate question in their lives.

Dr. Gary Habermas
Distinguished Professor of Apologetics and Philosophy
B.R. Lakin School of Theology, Liberty University

Dr. Harvey's courtroom drama is a fascinating and detailed look at the events and people around the crucifixion and resurrection, historically accurate and personally challenging.

Dr. Dennis Voskuil
DeWitt Professor of Church History
Western Theological Seminary, Holland, Michigan

No work affords a better nexus between the God-given emotions and intellect than does Jim Harvey's thoughtful and insightful exploration of the death and resurrection of Jesus.

Dr. William Brown
Psychologist, Author, and Clergyman
Chairman of TRT Inc.

In recent years we have often watched court room scenes in movies and on TV, where 'evidence' seemed to pile up and we found ourselves surprised when the facts were in, because some overlooked piece of evidence changed our mind. What is true of courtroom drama is also true in life. Multitudes of misinformed and biased people have silently formed conclusions on the resurrection without ever examining all the facts. Dr. Harvey takes the reader into a courtroom, where facts must be addressed, and calls witnesses to test the veracity of the resurrection. Unlike a sermon, which begins with certain assumed conclusions, the open courtroom environment Dr. Harvey creates encourages the reader to think, evaluate, and come to a well informed conclusion, namely that the evidence points to the reality of the literal, bodily resurrection of Jesus Christ. The witnesses and facts, independently and collectively, lead honest readers to that inevitable reality.

Rev. Thomas Couch
Pastor of Senior Adults
Calvary Church, Grand Rapids, Michigan

Acknowledgments

Many people are directly and indirectly responsible for this work. I would like to acknowledge and thank the following people: the Rev. Leonard Wezeman (deceased), who many years ago preached a series of sermons where he assumed the persona of a biblical character and brought them to life; Dr. Robert Sawyer, who encouraged the author to teach an adult Sunday School class on Easter Sunday morning, which focused on looking at the resurrection from the standpoint of reason, logic, and historical fact; Dr. Steve Nicholas, who after reading the first draft, encouraged the author to present a version of the book as a play for the first time.

Thanks also go to Mrs. Clothilda Harvey, an attorney, who read and critiqued the manuscript from the legal perspective. The Reverends Don Fulton, Hampton Morgan, and Dr. Bill Brown also reviewed and critiqued the manuscript as did Dr. William Brownson and Rev. Vern Hoffman of the Western Theological Seminary in Holland, Michigan. I sincerely appreciate their help and encouragement.

Special thanks are also due to the Rev. Mary Ann Pula, who directed the first production of the play, which was drawn from the book. The play entitled, "The Resurrection on Trial," is now published separately. Thanks also go to the first cast of the play, who gave of their time and wisdom to help shape the play and the book. These people were: Skip Abbitt, Dan Brooks, Linda Brubaker, Vic Govier,

Acknowledgements

Doug Harvey, Jackie Harvey, Pat Jones, Yvonne Maddox, Willie Miller, Jim Richardson, Elsie Taylor, Ralph Thomas III, Cam Weiffenbach, and Sue Wiffenbach. The play was first presented in the St. Paul's Moravian Church in Upper Marlboro, Maryland.

I also want to thank the Thursday Christian Men's Bible Study group in Grand Rapids Michigan led by Rick Awtrey. This group vetted the revised edition of the book and made a number of constructive suggestions for improvement. These men were Dan Borst, Roger Braybrook, Steve Cox, Dan Parker, Steve Pothoven, Jim Ribbens, Chuck Spliedt, Rob Umstead, Ed VerMurlen, and Jerry Ward.

Without the people above this work could have not reached its full development, and this author is grateful to each and every one for their input.

It is the author's sincerest wish that the reader would find in this work a new perspective on the momentous events of that Passover weekend nearly 2000 years ago, which changed the history of mankind.

L. James Harvey Ph.D.

Preface

Who was Jesus of Nazareth? This is a question people have debated since the first century. Who was this man who split history into before and after? Who, though he taught for only three years, is acknowledged to be one of the greatest teachers of all time? Whose symbol of his death, the cross, is probably the most recognized symbol in the world, found on buildings, in jewelry, in art, and in cemeteries around the globe? Who performed miracles and has changed the lives of millions? Was he just a man? Or was he much more?

Jesus is acknowledged by Jews to be a great teacher; by Moslems to be a great teacher and miracle worker, who was born of a virgin and went to heaven without dying; and by Christians as the Son of God and Savior. Yet the debate, as to who he really was, goes on and is usually heightened each Easter season, when the secular media search for new information, which might prove conclusively who he was.

We find a group of liberal theologians in a group called the Jesus Seminar studying scripture and voting on what they believe about Jesus and scripture. They have so far concluded about 80% of the New Testament is not true as written. More and more we hear liberal theologians like Bishop John Shelby Spong saying that Jesus did not really rise from the dead, but the disciples clearly thought he did. And so the debate goes on.

Preface

In his first letter to the Corinthians, the apostle Paul says (I Corinthians 15:14) "And if Christ has not been raised, your faith is futile; you are still in your sins" (New International Version). The King James Version says our faith is vain, if Christ is not risen. The issue of who Jesus of Nazareth was centers on the events that occurred on a Passover weekend in the year of 30AD. Did Jesus arise from the grave or not? If he did, then his claim to be the Son of God is believable. If he didn't, then he was mistaken about who he was, lied to his disciples, and is no different than other messianic impostors, who down through the years, have claimed to have the power to come back from the dead and couldn't.

In summary, the faith of the Christian centers on who Jesus was, and who he was centers on whether he arose from the grave and defeated death. Every Christian must decide for himself or herself who Jesus was. To not decide is to decide against. To decide he was a good man, but not a risen Savior is to, in Paul's words, have a faith that is vain and foolish.

This play is written to give the reader a new perspective and way to view of the circumstances that occurred on that fateful weekend in 30AD*, so each can make a clear informed decision and judge for himself or herself what really happened.

This work is well researched, critiqued, and it is historically and biblically correct. The author has been to Israel twice and has visited all of the places described in the book including the "Via

Dolorosa" and the two sites, which are held out as the likely places where Jesus was crucified and buried.

In short, based on the above the events portrayed here could have happened exactly as described. While some minor details may have been different, the primary events undoubtedly happened exactly as described. You will find detailed explanations for many of the events in the notes at the end of the book.

Since everyone must decide about what happened in 30 AD, the reader is asked to assume the role of a jury member when studying the evidence presented in the courtroom and to complete the jury ballot at the end of the trial.

Read with interest and attention to the facts presented in the trial and decide once and for all who this man Jesus of Nazareth really was.

*Note - Scholars do not all agree on the exact year of Jesus' crucifixion, however, the vast majority put it between 30AD and 33AD. The author uses 30AD with this understanding.

Table of Contents

Introduction

The American judicial system is called an adversarial system. It's called this because we believe the best way to determine truth and arrive at justice is to put the two sides to a dispute and into a competition, before an objective judge or jury, to see who can prevail in proving their case. Within the rules of evidence the sides battle each other to convince the judge and jury they have the truth on their side. This adversarial system has its flaws but, as a nation, we still believe it is the best way to find truth and justice.

In civil cases juries are told to make their decision based on the "preponderance of evidence." In short, if 51% of the evidence favors one side over the other, they are to vote for that side. In criminal cases we require a higher standard to protect against unjust convictions. In criminal cases we require proof "beyond reasonable doubt." In effect, Jurors are told they must vote not guilty, if they have a reasonable doubt the case against the accused is not true.

The American criminal justice system is used in this work as a vehicle for looking at and examining the facts surrounding the crucifixion and resurrection of Jesus. This venue gives us the opportunity to examine the major arguments for and against the resurrection in an interesting and meaningful way. The higher standard of proof "beyond reasonable doubt" is used.

Introduction

For purposes of this trial the Bible is assumed to be a book, which is historically accurate but not the Word of God. The Bible is therefore, used to help determine what happened in 30AD, but not who Jesus was - that is the reader's challenge. Other historical resources have also been used particularly secular books on the history of Rome and the Roman army. The author also studied major books arguing against the resurrection in order to build these arguments into the trial.

Authentic names have been used in the trial for all historical figures called to testify.

While not used as an exhibit in the trial, the author has provided a timeline exhibit at the end of the play, which the reader may find helpful in understanding the sequence of events of that fateful weekend in 30AD.

Come with me now to the court house in Grand Rapids, Michigan where the 17th Circuit Court is about to convene. Assume you have been selected to serve on the jury. Take the oath the judge administers, study the evidence carefully, listen to the arguments, hear the summations and judge's instructions, and render a verdict; because everyone living must ultimately decide who Jesus of Nazareth really was.

Trial

This is Lois Anderson of Channel 8 TV News reporting to you from outside the courthouse in Grand Rapids, Michigan, where a most unusual trial is about to begin. People have been lined up all night hoping to get the few available seats in the courtroom. Fortunately, Judge George Noteworthy has permitted our TV cameras to go into the courtroom, so we can bring you the entire trial. The court has spent a number of days selecting the jury, but they finished the selection process late last night, so the judge is ready to swear in the jury and alternates and begin hearing testimony this morning.

This is a most unusual case for two reasons. First, the question to be decided is not the typical guilt or innocence of a person charged with a crime. Rather the court processes will be used to resolve an issue, which mankind has debated for nearly 2000 years, namely did Jesus of Nazareth actually arise from the grave or did he not. Was he the Son of God or just another deluded individual who thought he was the Messiah, who the Bible prophesied was coming?

Second, the trial is unusual in that for the first time, because of modern technology, witnesses will be brought back from antiquity, who were there and observed the actual events. We have heard that Simon Peter, Caiaphas, and Pontius Pilate will be called.

Wait, I see one of the attorneys approaching. Let me see if I can get a word with him.

Anderson: Mr. Stockman! Mr. Stockman! May I have a word with you for our TV audience?

Stockman: Yes, but it will have to be brief the trial is about to begin.

Anderson: Thank you! Do you believe you will be able to prove the resurrection of Jesus was a hoax?

Stockman: Well, you must understand I don't have to prove anything. All I have to do is convince the jury there is reasonable doubt about the resurrection and that will be easy, because they will start with reasonable doubt.

Anderson: What do you mean?

Stockman: Well, no one on the jury has ever seen anyone rise from the dead, it just doesn't happen; therefore, they will come to the trial with doubts about the fact that anything like that could happen. My job is just to hold that position and keep them in that state of reasonable doubt. My opponent has a hopeless task of convincing them the impossible happened.

Anderson: One last question, Mr. Stockman, can you confirm the rumor that you will actually call Caiaphas, the high priest, to the stand?

Stockman: Yes, I can confirm that he is on the witness list, and I think you will find him a most powerful and persuasive witness.

Anderson: Thank you, Mr. Stockman. We will follow your case with interest. Oh, look, here comes the attorney for the people, who will try to prove that Jesus actually arose. Oh, Mr. Smith, Mr. Smith, may I have a brief word with you before you go into court.

Smith: Yes, but you will have to be brief.

Anderson: Thank you, Mr. Smith. Your opposing counsel, Mr. Stockman, just told us you have a hopeless task trying to prove Jesus arose from the dead, and that the jury comes to the case with reasonable doubt because they have never seen anyone arise from the dead. Isn't that true?

Smith: No! Not at all! We have spent days, as you know, selecting a jury. I believe we have people on the jury, who will keep an open mind. That's all I ask. It's true they have never seen anyone arise from the dead, but then they weren't there, and they have never confronted the kind of facts I will present to them. And, oh, yes, we will present first hand witnesses who were there and who did see what happened.

Anderson: Can you tell the audience who your first witness will be?

Smith: Yes, I plan to call Simon Peter, called the "Big Fisherman", and close follower of Jesus.

Anderson: Thank you, Mr. Smith. I can see you want to go in. So, there you have it. Both sides seem confident they will win the case. We have been informed the trial is about to begin, so we will now take you inside the courtroom. This is Lois Anderson for Channel 8 TV News.

Bailiff Johnson: All rise! The 17th Circuit Court of the State of Michigan is now in session, the Honorable George Noteworthy presiding.

Judge Noteworthy: Please be seated. I believe we are ready to proceed with the matter of whether Jesus of Nazareth arose from the dead. We have Mr. Robert Smith representing the people with the responsibility of proving Jesus of Nazareth rose from the dead. Mr. Daniel Stockman is the counsel for the defense. His responsibility is to demonstrate reasonable doubt as to whether this resurrection occurred. Are both counsels satisfied with the jury that has been selected and are you ready to proceed?

Mr. Smith and Mr. Stockman: Yes, we are your honor.

Judge Noteworthy: All right then I would like to ask the jury to stand, raise your right hands, and take the oath, as administered by the court clerk, Mrs. Jones.

Jones: Do you solemnly swear before God that you will hear the evidence in the case before you, that you will fairly and objectively consider all evidence presented, and that you will render a verdict according to the law and the instructions given to you by the court? If you are so minded please say, I will.

Jury: I will.

Judge Noteworthy: Be seated. Members of the jury we deeply appreciate your service in this most extraordinary trial. You will be asked to determine *beyond reasonable doubt* whether one, Jesus of Nazareth, actually rose from the dead or whether the story of his resurrection was a ruse perpetrated on history by his followers. Mr. Robert Smith, counsel for the people, will attempt to prove the resurrection true, based on the weight of evidence. The counsel for the defense, Mr. Daniel Stockman, will attempt to convince you the resurrection never occurred and, in fact, was a fraud and a hoax.

Because of the uniqueness of this trial some special rules will be in effect. Both sides have agreed they will each be allowed to call five witnesses from antiquity. Witnesses will be called in a rotating order with the people calling the first witness and the defense the second and so on. Each witness may be cross-examined once by the opposing counsel. No re-direct examination will be permitted. Following the ten witnesses each attorney will be allowed one summation. The defense will go first, with the people following. After the people's closing argument, I will instruct you on the law affecting the case. You may then deliberate as long as necessary, until you reach a verdict. You must reach a verdict! Because of the critical nature of this case, each of you must come to a conclusion on the matter. The court will not entertain a hung jury on this critical matter.

In this trial, because of its unusual character, hearsay evidence will be permitted as long as it is reasonable, directly related to the facts of the case, and not intended to emotionalize or distort the facts.

Now before we get to the opening statements and testimony I understand that both sides have agreed to a stipulation to be presented to the court. Is that true?

Attorneys: Yes, it is your honor.

Judge Noteworthy: For the benefit of the jury a stipulation or judicial notice is an agreement by both sides regarding the facts in a case. It is an agreement regarding facts that are not in dispute. It is a device used to make the judicial process more efficient and focused. In the judicial process when a stipulation or judicial notice is entered into the record, the jury is to consider the statement as fact, which is not subject to questioning in your deliberations. Please read the stipulation Mr. Smith.

Mr. Smith: Thank you your honor. In this case both sides agree to the facts as follows: We jointly agree that there was a historical figure by the name of Jesus of Nazareth. We further stipulate Jesus lived and taught in the land of Israel during the first century. Further we agree he was crucified by Pontius Pilate, the Roman procurator of Judea, in the year 30AD in Jerusalem on the day prior to the Jewish Sabbath, on which they celebrated the Passover Feast in that year. We also stipulate that Jesus was removed from the cross on that day prior to 6:00 PM, when the Jewish Sabbath began. Lastly we agree that the body of Jesus was missing on the third day following his crucifixion. *(See Note 1)*

Judge Noteworthy: Thank you Mr. Smith. Mr. Stockman do you agree to the facts as presented in the stipulation?

Mr. Stockman: Yes, I do your honor.

Judge Noteworthy: All right then, the court will take judicial notice of these facts and enter them in the court record. Are both counsels ready make your opening statements?

Both Counsels: Yes, we are your honor.

Judge Noteworthy: All right, Mr. Smith you may make your opening statement.

Mr. Smith: Ladies and Gentlemen of the jury I look forward to sharing this most important trial with you. Together we will search for truth about the most important event in the history of mankind. A few minutes ago you took a most important oath to objectively consider the evidence and to render a verdict based on it alone. All I ask of you is that you do exactly as you have promised.

Some feel I have an impossible task trying to prove a man rose from the dead because not one of us has seen such a thing or believe it is possible. You quite naturally come to the issue with an understandable doubt. But you come with something else that is critical namely your human experiences and a reason and logic to apply to the facts.

I submit that we will place irrefutable facts and information that will prove beyond reasonable doubt that Jesus of Nazareth was the Son of God and therefore had the power to rise from the grave – a power you and I and others do not have.

We will show how numerous prophesies made hundreds of years before his birth, by a number of different prophets, who did not know each other, foretold of Jesus' birth, life, death, and resurrection. We will show how the life of Jesus has affected the history of mankind as no other has. Jesus had a public ministry of less than 3 years, wrote no books or articles, led no armies, and headed no government yet his impact on history is greater than any other – could this be a coincidence? Or could it be that the maker of the universe did visit earth, as was predicted.

We will have the opportunity in this trial to hear from people who were there and who witnessed the events in 30AD. I only ask that you use your reason, logic, and human experience to ask whether they are telling the truth and whether their testimony rings true. If you will keep your minds open to the facts, we believe we will prove that Jesus was who he said he was and that he did what he said he would do. Ultimately you must decide whether Jesus was the Son of God, as he said he was, or whether he was a psychologically disturbed soul who thought he was God and got himself killed because of it. Could a psychologically disturbed individual have taught and impacted history as Jesus did? We believe ultimately you will find that harder to believe than that the Son of God arose from the grave. Please give our evidence a full and complete hearing. Thank you.

Judge Noteworthy: Thank you Mr. Smith. Mr. Stockman may we have your opening statement please?

Mr. Stockman: Yes, thank you, your honor. Ladies and gentlemen of the jury you have an awesome responsibility to make a decision on an issue that has divided people for two thousand years. Together we can put to rest the idea that Jesus rose from the grave. It is not possible for someone to do this and it never happened.

We will present evidence that will explain all of the facts in the case and show how the followers of Jesus conspired together to create a new religion in which they would be the leaders. Because of the heightened Jewish hope and awareness of the possible coming of a Messiah to relieve them from the Roman occupation, it was easy for Jesus to pretend he was the Messiah and to get people to follow him. Add a little magic and a little charisma and we get a leader who tried to start a new religion with him as the head. But he miscalculated and ended up dead.

We will show how Jesus died and will have testimony from the Roman Centurion who was there to certify the death. We will explain what happened to Jesus' body and how his followers craftily used the absence of the body to start a new religion with themselves as leaders.

Ladies and gentleman the fact is that men do not rise from the dead. We all know that. Jesus was a man and he died. That he died is a stipulated fact. I ask that you use your knowledge and common sense to reaffirm once and for all that Jesus died and stayed dead. All you need is reasonable doubt to vote against the resurrection. We will more than meet the burden of proving that there is more than reasonable doubt Jesus did not arise. It is a dead certain fact that he did not because no one could. Thank you.

Judge Noteworthy: All right, thank you counselor. I believe we are now ready to proceed with our first witness. Mr. Smith, call your first witness.

Mr. Smith: Your honor, the people call as their first witness Simon Peter.

Peter

Judge Noteworthy: Would the witness please face the court clerk and raise your right hand?

Mrs. Jones: Do you swear to tell the truth, the whole truth, and nothing but the truth, so help you God?

Peter: I do.

Judge Noteworthy: Please be seated and state your name for the court record.

Peter: My name is Simon Peter, but most people just call me by my surname Peter.

Mr. Smith: Good day, Peter.

Peter: Good day, sir.

Mr. Smith: Peter, how did you first come to know this man called Jesus of Nazareth?

Peter: Actually I came to know him because of my brother Andrew. Andrew had become a follower of a man called John the Baptist, who was preaching and baptizing people in a wilderness area beyond the River Jordan. John was telling about the coming of the Messiah, whom we Jews were looking for in fulfillment of numerous Old Testament prophesies. One day a man appeared on the shore of the Jordan River, while John was baptizing some believers, and John said, "Behold the lamb of God!" It was clear to Andrew that John was saying this man was the Messiah because there is clear reference in Isaiah 53 referring to the Messiah as a "lamb." Andrew and a friend left John the Baptist, with his blessing, and began following Jesus. My brother then contacted me and said I had to meet this Jesus, whom he believed to be the Promised One. I did, and, as you people like to say, the rest is history. I followed him as a disciple from the day I met him. *(See Note 2)*

Mr. Smith: Did you believe Jesus was the Messiah from the day you met him?

Peter: I can't say that I did, but I accepted the fact he could be and looked for proof that he was.

Mr. Smith: And did you find this proof?

Mr. Stockman: Your honor, I object to this line of questioning. Counsel is bolstering the credibility of Jesus. We are here to determine if Jesus arose from the grave not to discuss his character or whether he was the Messiah.

Mr. Smith: Your honor, our case hinges to a large extent on who Jesus was. It is foundational to our position that he was indeed the Son of God, and as such, had the power to do that, which a mere man could not do. This line of questioning is critical to our case.

Judge Noteworthy: I will overrule the objection, but I warn you, Mr. Smith, keep questions regarding the character of Jesus narrowly focused on that issue. If you stray at all, I will stop you and strike your remarks.

Mr. Smith: Thank you, your honor. Now Peter, You said you believed you had proof that Jesus was the Messiah. Can you tell us, please, what that proof was?

Peter: Well, it involved numerous things. First, John the Baptist said that was who he was, and John was considered by many to be a prophet of God. Also I had conversations with Jesus' mother Mary. She told of how an angel had appeared to her to tell her she was to bear the Messiah. She also told how she became pregnant, as a virgin, and bore Jesus in Bethlehem, and how an angel told her and Joseph to go into Egypt to escape the slaughter of children by Herod. She further told many remarkable things about Jesus as he grew up, such as his gaining great wisdom and knowledge, though he had no formal education. She told how, when he was 12, they found him in the Temple, sitting with the scholars, discussing deep religious matters. And these scholars were astonished by his wisdom. In effect, Mary confirmed that Jesus was far from an ordinary child. *(See Note 3)* But beyond this, I was perhaps closer to Jesus than any other human being. I saw him teach with such truth and insight, that he confounded the best scholars of the day. I saw him perform miracles healing the sick, feeding 5000 people, calming a storm, and even raising the dead, including Lazarus. And on the mount of transfiguration James, John, and I saw Jesus talking to Elijah and Moses. But the final piece of evidence, if I needed one, was his predicting his death and resurrection and appearing to us many times after his crucifixion. These things and others gave me proof beyond any doubt that Jesus was the Son of God and our Messiah. *(See Notes 4 and 5)*

Mr. Smith: Is there anything else?

Peter: Yes, there is one more point of importance. The Bible predicted the coming of the Messiah and Jesus fulfilled all of the prophecies.

Mr. Smith: Could you be more specific about this Peter?

Peter: Yes, our Holy Scriptures, written hundreds of years before the birth of Jesus, have many specific references to the coming of the

Messiah. There are at least 300 references to the Messiah and 61 very specific prophecies about his birth, life, and death, and Jesus fulfilled every one! *(See Note 6)*

Mr. Smith: Can you give me a specific example or two?

Peter: Yes, the Bible prophesies the Messiah will be born in Bethlehem, that he will be born of a virgin, that he will be of from the house of Jesse and of the lineage of King David.

Mr. Smith: Does Jesus fulfill these prophecies?

Peter: Yes, and over 50 others! No one else could possibly say that!

Mr. Stockman: Your honor, I object! The witness is stating facts not in evidence!

Judge Noteworthy: Sustained. Do you have evidence to support this statement counselor?

Mr. Smith: Yes, we do, your honor, I would like to introduce People's Exhibit #1 to make our point.

Judge Noteworthy: All right, we'll label this People's Exhibit #1.

Mr. Smith: Now, Peter, will you please explain this exhibit to the court?

Peter: Yes, a Peter Stoner, a statistician, calculated the probability that anyone could meet just 8 of these Biblical prophesies by chance alone. *(See Note 7)*

Mr. Smith: And what did he find?

Peter: He found that the chances of anyone meeting the 8 prophesies listed here, by chance alone, would be 1 in 10 to the 17th power or 1 in 100,000 trillions.

Mr. Stockman: Your honor, I object! This is not scientific proof! They are just some numbers someone dreamed up.

Mr. Smith: Your honor, statistics is an honored field of study and routinely used in scientific inquiry. In addition the American Scientific Affiliation, a recognized scientific association, has verified Mr. Stoner's work.

Judge Noteworthy: The objection is overruled. This information will be allowed into evidence!

Mr. Smith: Peter, let me clarify your testimony here. Are you saying that Jesus actually met all 61 specific biblical prophesies regarding the Messiah, but, if we took only the 8 stated here, the probability of anyone meeting them all by chance is 1 in 100,000 trillions?

Peter: Yes, that is exactly right. If we considered the probability of anyone meeting all 61 prophesies the numbers would be so high they would go out of sight. There is no question Jesus was the Messiah the Bible said would come!

Mr. Smith: Peter, I want to make this absolutely clear to the jury, so in summary I ask you again, is it your testimony that Jesus of Nazareth was an exceptional person, who in your opinion was the Son of God and the Messiah, whose coming was prophesied in the Old Testament and who is mentioned there some 300 times?

Peter: Yes this is my testimony.

Mr. Smith: Let us now turn our attention to the events surrounding the arrest, trial and crucifixion of Jesus. Your honor, I would like to introduce as People's Exhibit #2 a map of the Jerusalem area, as it was in 30 AD.

Judge Noteworthy: All right, the map will be labeled People's #2.

Peoples' Exhibit #1
Prophesies Regarding Jesus

Old Testament prophecies regarding the coming of the Messiah, which were fulfilled by Jesus and the likelihood such prophecies could have been fulfilled by chance alone.*

1. The Messiah would be born in Bethlehem (Micah 5:2)
2. The Messiah to be preceded by a messenger (Isaiah 40:3 and Malachi 3:1)
3. He would enter Jerusalem on the foal of donkey (Zechariah 9:9)
4. To be betrayed by a friend and be crucified (Psalm 41:9 and Psalm 55:12-14)
5. To be sold for 30 pieces of silver (Zechariah 11:12-13)
6. Betrayal money would be discarded and used for a potter's field (Zechariah 11:13)
7. He would not defend himself before his accusers (Isaiah 53:7)
8. To be pierced at death and crucified with thieves (Psalms 22:16, Zechariah 12:10, and Isaiah 53:12)

The chances of these 8 things happening to one person by chance are:

1 in 100,000 Trillions

*Note: From Science Speaks by Peter Stoner, Moody Press. Chicago,Illinois. 1963 (Used with their permission)

Peoples' Exhibit #2
Jerusalem in 30 AD

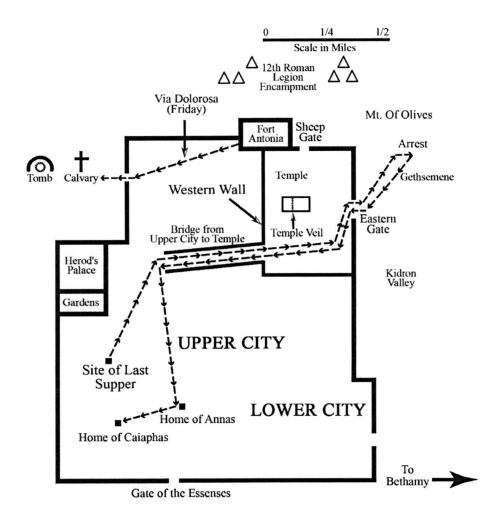

Jesus's Movements on Thursday – → – →

Mr. Smith: Peter, I understand you were with Jesus when the Temple Guard arrested him. *(See Note 8)*

Peter: Yes, I was. We had come from celebrating the Passover feast and our last supper with Jesus. We had gone with him to the Mt. of Olives, a short distance outside the eastern gate of Jerusalem, to a garden area called Gethsemane.

Mr. Smith: Peter, would you please show us on the map where these places are?

Peter: Yes, I'd be glad to. Here is where we had the last supper. We then went across the bridge from the upper city to the Temple. We then went through the Temple, out the eastern gate, and across the Valley Kidron to the Garden of Gethsemane, which is in an olive grove on the Mt. of Olives. Gethsemane is just a few hundred yards outside of the eastern gate.

Mr. Smith: Thank you. Why did you go there?

Peter: Jesus wanted some time alone to meditate and pray. He often went there. It is a quiet restful place overlooking the city of Jerusalem.

Mr. Smith: Please tell us what happened next.

Peter: Well, it got late. Some of us had fallen asleep, when we were awakened by the Temple Guard carrying torches and accompanied by Judas Iscariot. Judas came up and kissed Jesus on the cheek to identify him as the one the guards should arrest. I drew my sword and struck at Malcus, the servant of the high priest. He ducked his head and I cut off his ear. Jesus told me to put up my sword. He then picked up the ear and healed Malcus. *(See Notes 9 and 10)*

Mr. Smith: What happened next?

Peter: Seeing that Jesus wasn't going to use his supernatural power to defend himself, we became frightened. When one of the Temple Guards made a move to grab John, we panicked and ran away.

Mr. Smith: At about what time did the guards arrest Jesus?

Peter: It must have been about 11:00 or 11:30 PM. They wanted to arrest Jesus while the city was asleep and his many followers there would not interfere with their arrest.

Mr. Smith: What did you do after that?

Peter: When I found the guards were not chasing us, I decided to follow from a distance to see what would happen to Jesus. They took him first to Annas, a former high priest and important leader of the

Sanhedrin, for questioning, and then to Caiaphas, who was the current high priest. After some more questioning, Jesus was put on trial before the Sanhedrin, which was the high court with jurisdiction over Jewish secular and religious matters. This court found him guilty of blasphemy and condemned him to death. Shortly after dawn the Sanhedrin met again, more formally, and confirmed the verdict of the earlier trial. Then Jesus was taken to Pontius Pilate, the Roman Procurator of Judea, in order to have the death sentence ratified, since Rome had earlier taken away the Jewish authority to carry out capital punishment. I understand Pilate examined him and sent him to Herod and that Herod examined him and sent him back to Pilate. I was certain that Caiaphas and his cronies would succeed in having Jesus crucified, so I left and went to my quarters to try and sort out what to do next. *(See Note 9)*

Mr. Smith: Were you at the crucifixion?

Peter: No, I couldn't bear to see Jesus suffer like that plus I was afraid they would identify me as one of his followers and arrest me. John, with whom I was staying, went to be with Mary, the mother of Jesus, when we finally heard they were indeed going to crucify him. John was younger looking and would not likely be identified as a follower of Jesus.

Mr. Smith: Did anything unusual happen that day?

Peter: Yes, sometime after Jesus was nailed to the cross, around 12 noon, an eerie darkness fell over the area. Later there was an earthquake, and I understand the veil in the Temple was split in two. I also understand that some people who had been dead for some time came out of their graves and appeared to friends in the city. *(See Note 12)*

Mr. Stockman: Your honor, I object to these later two comments as inadmissible hearsay evidence.

Judge Noteworthy: The objection is sustained. The jury will disregard the statements regarding the veil of the Temple and the appearance of the dead, neither of which the witness experienced personally. His comments regarding the darkness and the earthquake are received in evidence because he personally experienced them. *(See Note 13)*

Mr. Smith: Peter, let me now turn to the events that occurred on the first day of the week following the crucifixion of Jesus. I assume you observed the Jewish Sabbath, as you normally would have.

Peter: That is correct, Mr. Smith.

Mr. Smith: Tell us what happened after the Sabbath ended.

Peter: Shortly after sunrise on the first day of the week Mary Magdalene came rushing to our quarters out of breath and said that someone had taken the body of Jesus from the tomb. Upon hearing this, John and I started running toward the tomb, which was not far away. John, who is younger and faster than I, arrived first and waited outside. When I arrived, I found the stone, covering the entrance, had been moved away. I immediately went in to see if the body was there. *(See Note 14)*

Mr. Smith: And was the body there?

Peter: No, it was gone, as Mary had said, but we did find the grave clothes and in a very strange position. *(See Note 15)*

Mr. Smith: What do you mean in a strange position?

Peter: The grave clothes laid where the body had been, as if the body had just vanished from inside them without their having been un-wrapped. The napkin, which had been about the head, was neatly rolled up and left nearby.

Mr. Smith: Did you believe at this point that Jesus had risen from the dead?

Peter: I didn't know what to believe. The body was gone, but who would take it? And if someone did take it, why would they leave the grave clothes? And how could they get the body out without unwrapping it? I was confused, and even though Jesus had told us several times he would rise from the dead on the third day, I was not sure that had happened, because it is not common to human experience.

Mr. Smith: Peter are you sure you went to the right tomb? Is it possible you made a mistake and went to a new tomb prepared for someone else?

Peter: That's not possible. Mary Magdalene and John were at the crucifixion, with the mother of Jesus, and they remained until Joseph of Arimathaea prepared the body of Jesus for burial. The grave is only a matter of a hundred yards or so from the hill of crucifixion, so they saw Jesus placed in the tomb. There could be no mistake. Beside the grave clothes were there. No, there was no mistake, this was the new tomb of Joseph of Arimathaea where Jesus had been placed, and which had been sealed by the Roman guard. *(See Note 16)*

Mr. Smith: What did you do next Peter?

Peter: We went back to our quarters and told the others what had happened. Not long after some women, who had gone to the tomb to anoint the body of Jesus, came to us and said they had seen Jesus and he was alive! Then Mary Magdalene, who had followed us back to the tomb, said she too had seen Jesus alive.

Mr. Smith: They said they saw Jesus alive?

Peter: Yes, and then he appeared to me also!

Mr. Smith: You saw Jesus as well?

Peter: Yes, while I was alone, Jesus appeared to me. He showed me his nail prints to prove he was alive. He then asked me to gather the disciples together that evening. *(See Note 17)*

Mr. Smith: What happened next?

Peter: Later that afternoon two followers of Jesus, who had been on the road to Emmaus, said that Jesus had joined them in their journey, though they did not realize at first it was Jesus. I then got all the disciples who were in the area together. There were 10 of us; Thomas was not there and Judas had killed himself. As we were having dinner, it happened. Jesus appeared to all of us. He just suddenly was there. He didn't come in through the door, which was closed. We were afraid at first, supposing this to be a spirit or an angel, then he said, "Peace be unto you". We recognized the voice and knew immediately it was Jesus. He then showed his scars to the others, as he had to me. From that point on there was no question in our minds. We all knew he had truly risen.

Mr. Smith: Let me clarify this point. Is it your testimony that you and the other disciples only believed Jesus had really risen when he showed you the scars he had from the crucifixion?

Peter: That is correct. After all for a person to rise from the dead is contrary to human reason, and even though Jesus told us several times it would happen, I don't believe we actually thought it would.

Mr. Smith: And did you ever see Jesus again?

Peter: Yes, on several occasions. For a period of 40 days he made appearances, at one time to 500 of our brethren. Then he made a final appearance to us on the Mt. of Olives and made his final ascension to heaven. *(See Note 18)*

Mr. Smith: How many times did you see Jesus after his crucifixion?

Peter: I personally saw him at least 6 times.

Mr. Smith: Let us be clear about this Peter, is it your testimony to this jury that you saw Jesus of Nazareth alive on 6 occasions after he was crucified?

Peter: Yes, that is my testimony and it is the truth.

Mr. Smith: Peter, the explanation given for the empty tomb by some, is that Jesus' followers stole the body to prove Jesus had risen. In light of that I ask you these questions: Did you or any of the disciples break the Roman seal on the tomb?

Peter: No, we did not!

Mr. Smith: Did you or any of the disciples enter the tomb and take the body of Jesus?

Peter: No, we did not! The tomb was sealed and guarded by Roman soldiers.

Mr. Smith: Peter, were you, or to your knowledge, any other follow-ers of Jesus, ever accused or questioned by the authorities about stealing the body of Jesus?

Peter: No, never. I was arrested with John some months later for teaching the people in Jerusalem that Jesus was the Christ, and that he had arisen from the dead, but the authorities never asked me anything about stealing the body. *(See Note 19)*

Mr. Smith: Let me clarify this point then, because it is critical. Is it true, according to your knowledge, that no follower of Jesus was ever questioned, accused, or convicted of breaking the seal on the tomb and taking the body of Jesus?

Peter: That is correct! To my knowledge no one was.

Mr. Smith: Peter, let me ask you about something I have wondered about. I understand that the Romans executed you because you were a Christian.

Peter: That is correct. I was in Rome when the great fire occurred in 64 AD. Nero, the emperor, found it convenient to blame the Christians for the fire and a fierce persecution took place. I was arrested along with Paul and many others. Paul was beheaded, as Roman citizens were, but most of us were crucified, as Jesus had been. *(See Note 20)*

Mr. Smith: Tradition has it that you requested to be crucified upside down because you felt you were unworthy to die in the same position that Jesus had. Is this true?

Peter: No, it is not true. It is true I felt unworthy to die as Jesus had, but, if you knew the Romans, you would know they wouldn't respond to a request such as that from a Christian particularly. It would have caused them some extra work. Crucifying someone upside down would have been very difficult for them to do. No, they would not have granted that kind of request. They only knew one way to crucify their enemies and that was as Jesus had died.

Mr. Smith: One last question, Peter. On the night Jesus was arrested you ran away in fear and yet later you preached the Christian message, even though you knew you could be arrested and killed. What made the difference between the fear at Gethsemane and the courage you later exhibited?

Peter: The resurrection and the coming of the Holy Spirit some days later at Pentecost. After those events I knew beyond doubt after that Jesus was the Messiah.

Mr. Smith: Thank You for your testimony. I have no further questions.

Judge Noteworthy: He is your witness Mr. Stockman. You may cross-examine.

Mr. Stockman: Thank you, your honor. Good day, Peter.

Peter: Good day, Mr. Stockman.

Mr. Stockman: Peter isn't it true that on the night Jesus was arrested you denied that you knew him?

Peter: Your honor, do I have to answer that question?

Judge Noteworthy: I'm afraid you do Peter. You are under oath and, since you cannot be prosecuted for any criminal act by our courts. You do not have a Fifth Amendment privilege. Please answer the question.

Peter: Then, the answer is, yes.

Mr. Stockman: Isn't it true Peter, that you not only denied you knew Jesus once, but you denied you knew him three times. *(See Note 21)*

Peter: Yes, but I was afraid I would be arrested and tried along with Jesus. Caiaphas and his cronies wanted this new religious movement stopped at all costs. We were a serious threat to him.

Mr. Stockman: Your honor, I object to the witness's response and move that all of his answer be stricken, following his yes response.

Judge Noteworthy: Your objection is sustained. Peter, I must caution you to answer the questions simply and to refrain from speculating about the motives of others. Please continue counselor.

Mr. Stockman: Thank you, your honor. So Peter, you want this jury to believe you were a close friend of this Jesus, when you admit you denied even knowing him at least three times the night of his arrest?

Peter: It is the truth. Nothing makes me sadder than to remember my weakness and denial of Jesus in his darkest hour.

Mr. Stockman: Now, let me ask some questions about this so-called resurrection. Isn't it true you were not at the crucifixion and did not see where Jesus was buried?

Peter: That's true.

Mr. Stockman: Isn't it also true that on the first day of the week you went to the wrong tomb and in fact to a new tomb that was being prepared for the burial of someone else?

Peter: No, that is not true. I went with John. He had seen where Jesus was buried on Friday. Besides, we found the grave clothes and the broken Roman seal. No, there is no question we went to the right tomb. *(See Note 22)*

Mr. Stockman: Isn't it also true, Peter, that you stole the body of Jesus, so you could tell people he arose and become the leader of a new religious movement?

Peter: How could we steal the body, if, as you say, we didn't know where the grave was?

Mr. Stockman: I'm the one who asks the questions. Please just answer them! I remind you Peter you are under oath, and I ask you again, didn't you or some other followers of Jesus steal his body in order to create the illusion he had risen from the dead, as he said he would?

Peter: No, neither I nor anyone else stole the body. Jesus actually physically arose from the dead.

Mr. Stockman: Isn't it also true, Peter, that Jesus of Nazareth wanted to start a new religion with himself as the head? And didn't he promise you that you would be an important leader in this new religion?

Peter: Jesus never wanted to start a new religion. He saw himself as the fulfillment of biblical prophecy and a continuation of the traditional faith. He did give me major responsibility for his followers and for spreading the truth, but I did not seek to be a religious leader as you imply. *(See Note 23)*

Mr. Stockman: But didn't Jesus criticize the religious leaders and try to lead people away from them.

Peter: Jesus was very critical of the religious leaders for establishing so many rules and regulations that their legalism distorted the true faith. They had squeezed all the joy and love out. This made a loving God seem like a cruel tyrant just waiting for people to make a mistake, so he could punish them. Jesus pointed people to a loving God who wanted people to succeed. A God whose laws were to guide people through a difficult life, not set them up to be punished. No, Jesus wanted to correct the traditional faith, which had been turned into something God never intended. Jesus did not try to lead people away from their traditional faith and set up a new religion. He wanted more than anything for the religious leaders to see the error of their ways and change.

Mr. Stockman: But didn't Jesus' actions lead to a new religion? And weren't you rewarded by becoming a leader in it?

Peter: We did not intend to start a new religion. Jesus was the fulfillment of biblical prophesies. It was the failure of the Jewish religious leaders to recognize the Messiah and to reform our faith that caused a split. The true faith even today sees its roots go back through the Old Testament to Adam and Eve, our first parents. We have deep hopes that the day will still come when all those of the Jewish faith will accept Jesus as the Messiah and follow his leading. As you may know, there is evidence, even now in the 21st century, that many Jews are recognizing Jesus as the Messiah. There is a growing Jews for Jesus movement.

As to my becoming a leader in this movement, yes, Jesus gave me some special leadership responsibilities. But, I did not profit from this as you imply. I gave my life for the truth Jesus taught us. I was imprisoned more than once, beaten, and away from my family far more than

I wanted. Jesus taught us to be frugal and to live humbly. None of us ever got rich or tried to set ourselves up as leaders to whom homage or a large salary was due. If I had wanted a softer life, I would have stayed at home and continued fishing on the Sea of Galilee. My family had wealth and servants. I gave that up to follow a risen Christ.

Mr. Stockman: I have no further questions your honor.

Judge Noteworthy: All right Mr. Stockman, according to our agreement you may call your first witness for the defense.

Mr. Stockman: Your honor, I call Joseph Caiaphas to the stand.

Caiaphas

Judge Noteworthy: The witness will please face the court clerk and raise his right hand.

Mrs. Jones: Do you swear to tell the truth, the whole truth, and nothing but the truth, so help you God?

Caiaphas: I do.

Mr. Stockman: Caiaphas, would you please tell the court what your position was in 30AD.

Caiaphas: I was the High Priest of the Jews in the Temple in Jerusalem.

Mr. Stockman: And are you also a Sadducee? *(See Note 22)*

Caiaphas: That is correct. We differ from the Pharisees in that we do not believe there is a heaven or a life after death.

Mr. Stockman: Did you know a man called Jesus of Nazareth?

Caiaphas: Yes, all too well.

Mr. Stockman: Please tell me about your relationship with him.

Caiaphas: He was a troublemaker we had to eliminate to save the Jewish people and our faith. Jesus was a rabbi who was fomenting false teaching and gathering a following of people who were a threat to start a revolt against Rome.

Mr. Stockman: So, in your judgment Jesus was stirring up a revolt?

Caiaphas: Yes. Many of our people were following him. They believed he was healing people and performing miracles. They even believed he had raised a man named Lazarus from the dead. Some also believed a strange preacher named John the Baptist, when he said Jesus was the long awaited Jewish Messiah. About a week before we put Jesus on trial he was welcomed into Jerusalem by the people, as a king. We knew if we didn't stop him we were headed for big trouble.

Mr. Stockman: What kind of trouble?

Caiaphas: We were afraid the followers of Jesus would start an armed revolt to throw off Roman occupation. We had carefully developed a reasonable working relationship with Rome, and a revolt would have led to a terrible purge by them. The Romans are merciless when crossed. Many Jews would have died in a revolt, our Temple would probably be closed or worse and everything we had gained could have been lost. As you know, this actually did happen 40 years later, and our Holy Temple was totally destroyed. Jesus was also undermining our Jewish faith with his teaching. He was questioning our Sabbath laws and our understanding of the law in general. He was turning people against us, as religious leaders, and questioning many of our interpretations of God's word.

Mr. Stockman: So you felt you had to remove him?

Caiaphas: Yes, and I wasn't the only one. A large majority of the Sanhedrin also felt it was better to eliminate one man than to risk a revolt that would kill hundreds or thousands of Jews.

Mr. Stockman: Tell me in some detail how you managed to remove this threat to the Jewish nation.

Mr. Smith: Your honor, I object to counsel's description of Jesus, as a threat to the nation. There is no evidence of this at all.

Judge Noteworthy: The objection is sustained. Save your editorializing for your summation Mr. Stockman. The jury is instructed to disregard counsel's statement regarding Jesus as a threat to the nation.

Mr. Stockman: Caiaphas, please tell us about the events that led to the trial and conviction of Jesus.

Caiaphas: When we had decided Jesus must be neutralized, we looked for a possible way to take him and try him without stirring up his followers in Jerusalem. By our good fortune one of Jesus' followers, named Judas Iscariot, came to us and offered to help us, for a price, of course. He was disaffected with this Jesus for some reason. He agreed to let us know when we might arrest Jesus without stirring up a crowd. At about 8:00PM on the Thursday before Passover Judas came and told me that later that night Jesus would be on the Mt. of Olives with about 10 followers and we could take him easily, while the city was asleep. I decided to arrest Jesus and try him that night, so we could have the Sanhedrin act at first light, and we could have Pilate affirm the sentence early Friday morning. If we could do this, we could crucify Jesus and have it all done before the Sabbath began that night and before the followers of Jesus could organize to stop us *(See Note 24)*

Mr. Stockman: And did things work out as planned?

Caiaphas: Yes, but with a couple of hitches. Judas led our Chief Captain and a squad of our Temple guards to the Garden of Gethsemene on the Mt. of Olives and we captured him about 11:30PM that night without any trouble. The few followers with Jesus fled, when they saw Jesus was not going to resist arrest. They brought Jesus to Annas, the former High Priest, and then to my house, where I had convened a meeting of key religious leaders from among the Scribes and Pharisees, who made up the Sanhedrin. We put Jesus on trial before the High Court and we convicted him. I then called a formal meeting of the Sanhedrin for 7:30AM, so we could validate the verdict.

Mr. Stockman: Were you able to get all members of the Sanhedrin on such short notice? And could you get the necessary witnesses that night for the court trial?

Caiaphas: Well, a few members of the Sanhedrin couldn't be located. I believe at least one was out of Jerusalem at the time. We did find witnesses, but we couldn't find two who could agree, fortunately, however, as it turned out, we didn't need them.

Mr. Stockman: What do you mean you didn't need them?

Caiaphas: After the trial had gone on for some time, with no progress at all, I finally became upset and just flat out asked Jesus, if, by the living God, he was the Christ, the Son of God. And he said, and I'll never forget his exact words, " I am: and you will see the Son of man sitting at the right hand of power and coming on the clouds of heaven." Well, when I heard this blasphemy, I tore my clothes to purify myself in the face of this irreverent affront to God. I knew we had him too, since by his own words he committed blasphemy in front of the Sanhedrin, an offense punishable by death under our law.

(See Note 24)

Mr. Stockman: So, the Sanhedrin convicted Jesus and sentenced him to death and the Sanhedrin validated the action at their meeting early on that Friday morning.

Caiaphas: Yes, and fortunately the night before, I had told Pilate we would like to have him review a sentence early that morning; and he had agreed to set time aside for us. *(See Note 26)*

Mr. Stockman: So, you took him to Pilate to have your death sentence affirmed. And this, I understand, was because Rome had taken away your authority to execute prisoners.

Caiaphas: Yes.

Mr. Stockman: And did he affirm your sentence?

Caiaphas: Well, yes, but here we had a problem. When we got there, Pilate took Jesus inside Fort Antonia to examine him. We couldn't go in or we would have been defiled before the Passover, so we waited outside. After a time Pilate came out and said he had found out Jesus was a Galilean and since Herod, who had authority over Galilee, was in Jerusalem for the Passover, he would send him to Herod to be judged. So, Jesus was taken to Herod's Palace and was examined there.

For some reason Pilate did not want to accept responsibility for Jesus and must have hoped Herod would condemn him. Herod had heard of Jesus, and his miracles, and wanted Jesus to perform for him. But Jesus stood mute. In spite of Herod's requests for some miracles, he did nothing. And, when the accusations we brought against him were presented, Jesus said nothing. Herod finally gave up saying he could find no offense Jesus had committed. Herod's soldiers mocked and beat Jesus and then took him back to Pilate. *(See Note 27)*

Mr. Stockman: Did Pilate then affirm your sentence?

Caiaphas: Yes, but not without difficulty. Pilate told me later that his wife, Claudia Procula had sent him a message to have nothing to do with Jesus. She claimed to have had a dream, in which she saw that Jesus was innocent, and that Pilate would be in trouble, if he condemned him. Finally, Pilate thought he had found a way out. He remembered at Passover it was the custom to release a prisoner to the people as a sign of good will. So Pilate asked the people who they would like released, Jesus or Barabbas. Barabbas had been convicted of murder not long before. The people responded forcefully that they wanted Barabbas released. Pilate at this point affirmed our sentence and turned Jesus over to the Roman Legion to be scourged and crucified. *(See Note 28)*

Mr. Stockman: And was the sentence carried out?

Caiaphas: Yes, Jesus and two other criminals were crucified around mid morning on that Friday.

Mr. Stockman: Did you make any other requests to Pilate regarding Jesus?

Caiaphas: Yes, there were three. One related to a sign placed over the head of Jesus. As you may know, the Romans put a notice above the head of those they execute so any one passing by will know why a person is dying. Pilate had them put a sign over Jesus saying "King of the Jews." I was furious. I told Pilate it should say, "He said he was King of the Jews." But Pilate wouldn't change it. Later that afternoon I sent a request that the legs of those who had been crucified be broken to hasten death so they could be buried before the start of the Sabbath and Passover celebration which began at 6:00PM that day. The third request I made the next day around mid-day, I went to Pilate and asked him to seal Jesus' tomb and to place a guard over it for 48 hours. *(See Note 29)*

Mr. Stockman: Why did you ask for the seal and guard?

Caiaphas: We remembered that Jesus had said he would be killed and that he would rise on the third day. I wanted to make sure his followers did not steal the body, so they could falsely claim he had risen.

Mr. Stockman: Did Pilate agree to your requests to hasten the death of those who were crucified and did he give you the seal and guard?

Caiaphas: Yes, the legs of both thieves were broken, but I understand Jesus was already dead, so they did not break his legs. The centurion said they had pierced Jesus' side and found water with the blood indicating he was dead. *(See Note 30)* Pilate then wrote out an order for the sealing of the tomb and a guard. The order was given to Centurion Petronius for execution.

Mr. Stockman: And did the Centurion execute the order?

Caiaphas: Yes, the tomb was sealed and a guard was posted. Centurion Petronius over saw to it all himself and he took personal command of the guard.

Mr. Stockman: Caiaphas, would you please tell the jury what it meant to seal the tomb.

Caiaphas: Yes, a cord is passed across the stone in front of the tomb. It is then attached to the sides of the tomb with sealing clay. As the clay dries an impression is made in it with the seal of the Emperor. Everyone then knows that to willfully break the seal without the permission of the Procurator, the Roman ruler in the area, is to commit an act punishable by death.

Mr. Stockman: So, the tomb of this Jesus was sealed on Saturday afternoon and a Roman guard was placed around the tomb.

Caiaphas: That is correct.

Mr. Stockman: Please tell the jury what happened next.

Caiaphas: At about 5:00AM on the first day of the week, my servant awakened me and said a Roman centurion and his men were outside and wanted to talk to me.

Mr. Stockman: And what happened next?

Caiaphas: The centurion was Petronius, who had commanded the guard at the tomb. He told a story that was surprising.

Mr. Stockman: Please tell the jury what the centurion said.

Caiaphas: He said that around 4:00AM a light appeared around the tomb. At the same time there was a rolling earthquake. He said he and his men were frozen, so they couldn't move. A light surrounded the tomb entrance and was strange in that, while it was bright it, did not hurt the eyes to look at it. It also had a soft gentle calm about it. While he and his men were startled and frozen, they were not frightened because of the soft quality of the light. He said it must have been there for 15 to 20 minutes. They also saw a figure come out of the light, break the seal, and roll the stone away. Then they saw a figure come out of the tomb. When the light disappeared and he and his men could move, they found the body of Jesus was gone. He came straight to my home to report this to me, because he knew of my interest in the matter. *(See Note 31)*

Mr. Stockman: And what did you do next?

Caiaphas: Since we couldn't explain what had happened, and we knew people would soon find out the body of Jesus was not in the tomb, we decided to agree on a story we could tell to explain the body's disappearance. We agreed we would tell anyone who asked that the followers of Jesus had stolen his body, while the guards slept. I agreed to intercede with Pilate, if he decided to punish the guard for sleeping and for failing in their mission. *(See Note 32)*

Mr. Stockman: Do you believe Jesus' followers stole his body?

Caiaphas: I'm not sure, but they must have. It's the only logical explanation for what happened.

Mr. Smith: Your honor, I object, the witness is expressing an opinion for which he has produced no evidence.

Judge Noteworthy: Caiaphas, do you have evidence the body was stolen?

Caiaphas: Well, not what you would call evidence, I guess.

Judge Noteworthy: Then the objection is sustained. The jury will disregard the witness' comment regarding the stealing of the body of Jesus. Please continue Mr. Stockman.

Mr. Stockman: Did Pilate ever question what had happened?

Caiaphas: Not to my knowledge.

Mr. Stockman: Did Jesus' followers have anything to say about what happened?

Caiaphas: Yes, my worst fears came true. They claimed he had risen from the grave. And a number of them said they had seen him in person. Not long after Peter and John, two of Jesus disciples, were preaching in the Temple that Jesus had risen and in so doing proved he was the Messiah. We warned them to stop, but they just continued. Finally, a couple of months after the crucifixion we had to arrest them both and put them in prison.

Mr. Stockman: Caiaphas, let me see if I can sum up your position on this. Is it your position that the followers of Jesus pulled off some type of magical trick to distract the Roman soldiers, and then stole the body of Jesus, so they could say he was resurrected and was truly the Messiah? And furthermore did this, so they could get people to join their religious sect?

Caiaphas: Yes, that is my testimony. I couldn't have said it better.

Mr. Stockman: I have no further questions. He's your witness.

Judge Noteworthy: Mr. Smith, you may cross-examine.

Mr. Smith: Thank you, your honor. Now Caiaphas, let me ask you about the arrest and trial of Jesus. You say he was arrested at about 11:30PM and that members of the Sanhedrin who had gathered at your home tried him that night?

Caiaphas: That's correct.

Mr. Smith: Is it not True that your law requires the calling of witnesses and that at least two of them must agree, as to the offense, or you cannot convict a prisoner? *(See Note 33)*
Caiaphas: That's right.

Mr. Smith: And did you call witnesses in the middle of the night, who could agree and convict Jesus?

Caiaphas: We called several witnesses, but they couldn't agree; as it turned out we didn't need them since he convicted himself with his own words, as I have testified.

Mr. Smith: Based on a question you asked as presiding judge of the court?

Caiaphas: Yes.

Mr. Smith: Isn't it contrary to your court procedure for the judge to question a defendant?

Caiaphas: Well, usually we don't do it, but this was an exceptional case.

Mr. Smith: Please answer yes or no sir. Isn't it a violation of your court procedures for a judge to question a defendant?

Caiaphas: Normally, yes.

Mr. Smith: Did any witness testify that Jesus had ever talked about or sought to plot a revolt against the Romans?

Caiaphas: No, we convicted him for blasphemy, as I have testified.

Mr. Smith: Is blasphemy a violation of Roman law?

Caiaphas: No, they have no respect for our faith. It is a most serious violation of our religious laws, however. It is, of course, an affront to their emperor, who believes he is the supreme ruler and a god.

Mr. Smith: Caiaphas, if Jesus was the Son of God and the Messiah, then what he said in your court was the truth, and not blasphemy, isn't that true?

Caiaphas: Technically you are right, but we knew he was not the Messiah.

Mr. Smith: Let me return to the trial. Isn't it a violation of your law to have a trial involving capital punishment at night?

Caiaphas: Yes, but technically the verdict of the trial was affirmed about 7:30 AM in the morning, so this is just a technicality. Actually the Sanhedrin officially delivered the verdict in the morning, making it legal. *(See Note 33)*

Mr. Smith: Isn't it also true that under your law the High Priest must fast and pray for 24 hours before a death sentence can be reaffirmed and carried out?

Caiaphas: That's true, but technically it wasn't required here because it was only Pilate who could give the death sentence, therefore, the Sanhedrin was only recommending an action not taking it themselves.

Mr. Smith: Caiaphas, under your law isn't it necessary for a person to invoke the name of God in order to commit blasphemy?

Caiaphas: Yes, it is.

Mr. Smith: Isn't it also true, by your own testimony, that Jesus did not invoke the name of God in his statement therefore under your law he did not commit blasphemy?

Caiaphas: That's not true. In my question to him I invoked the name of God and when he answered Jesus accepted my statement thereby by inference invoking the name of God and making it blasphemy

Mr. Smith: Caiaphas, there's another of your technicalities. It is clear to anyone who objectively reviews the facts of this matter that you prejudged Jesus, had him convicted illegally and arranged to have him killed though he was totally innocent of all wrong doing.

Caiaphas: That's' not true.

Mr. Smith: Didn't you testify you had contacted Pilate even before Jesus was arrested and asked him to set aside time early the next morning to review your verdict? Doesn't this prove you already believed he would be found guilty and be sentenced to death?

Caiaphas: I thought he might be; and I wanted to be prepared in case he was. We could have canceled the appointment with Pilate, if he had been innocent. Besides, if he was guilty, as I thought, we had to have the sentence executed before Jesus' followers could organize an armed revolt to free him.

Mr. Smith: Isn't it true that neither Pilate nor Herod found any fault with Jesus, certainly nothing remotely requiring a death penalty?

Caiaphas: That's true; Pilate didn't see the danger.

Mr. Smith: What danger? Wasn't the danger that your phony laws would be exposed and your power base threatened?

Mr. Stockman: I object, your honor, counsel is badgering the witness.

Judge Noteworthy: The objection is sustained. Save your editorial comments for your summation Mr. Smith.

Mr. Smith: Yes, your honor. Caiaphas, isn't it true that when Jesus came back from Herod, and it looked like Pilate would not affirm your verdict, you actually blackmailed Pilate? *(See Note 34)*

Caiaphas: I didn't blackmail him, I just reminded him, that if he did not affirm our verdict on Jesus, we had the right to take our case to Tiberius the emperor.

Mr. Smith: This is something you have done before isn't it?

Caiaphas: Yes, not long ago Pilate illegally took some of our Temple funds to build an aqueduct into Jerusalem. We took the matter all the way to Tiberius, and we won. Tiberius just wants peace and quiet in the colonies plus his taxes, of course. He doesn't want to make us unhappy or to incite us to riot. So he overruled Pilate, and made him return the funds.

Mr. Smith: So knowing you had already embarrassed Pilate before Tiberius, you threatened to do it again, didn't you?

Caiaphas: He embarrassed himself with an illegal action. In the case of Jesus, I was sure I could convince Tiberius that Pilate was risking a revolt in Judea and Galilee, if Jesus wasn't executed.

Mr. Smith: Even this nearly failed didn't it?

Caiaphas: Yes, Pilate's wife Claudia got to him. She was convinced bad things would happen to Pilate, if he convicted Jesus. Pilate tried his best to release Jesus. He would have let Jesus go instead of Barabbas, if I hadn't anticipated a problem and packed the courtyard with my people. It was in the courtyard of Fort Antonia, where Pilate asked the people who they wanted released. When he asked the crowd my followers outnumbered all others and made sure Jesus was the one who would die.

Mr. Smith: Let me summarize this, Caiaphas. You had Jesus arrested late at night. You managed to have Jesus convicted without witnesses, and have his conviction confirmed by the Sanhedrin at dawn. You then managed to have Pilate affirm your verdict, even though neither Pilate nor Herod saw any fault in him. That's quite a fete. You send an innocent man to death in less than 14 hours and say you did it within the law.

Caiaphas: I did, but he was guilty not innocent. I saved our faith and our country.

Mr. Smith: That's your opinion sir; you sent an innocent man to his death. But let me switch the focus to the empty tomb. When Petronius and the soldiers came to you, did they not tell you of a miraculous event at the tomb?

Caiaphas: It was unusual but not miraculous.

Mr. Smith: Can you explain what happened?

Caiaphas: No, but there has to be a logical explanation.

Mr. Smith: Did you know for a fact that Jesus' followers took his body?

Caiaphas: No, but that is the only logical explanation.

Mr. Smith: Couldn't Jesus have arisen from the dead through the power of God, and then appeared to his followers, as they said?

Caiaphas: No, this can't happen. There is no spirit world out there; there is no life after death. We Sadducees are certain of it.

Mr. Smith: Isn't it true you bribed Petronius and his soldiers to tell people Jesus' followers stole body while they slept? And didn't you promise to intercede with Pilate, if their actions were questioned?

Caiaphas: I gave them some money and they agreed to tell the story of Jesus body being stolen. It wasn't a bribe, since I am sure that is what happened.

Mr. Smith: There is no evidence, sir, that the body was stolen. You may be the only one close to these events who thinks so.

Mr. Stockman: There he goes again, your honor.

Mr. Smith: I'm sorry, your honor. I withdraw my last statement.

Judge Noteworthy: Thank you counsel. Are you through with this witness?

Mr. Smith: No, I have one or two more questions. Caiaphas, if you were certain Jesus' followers had stolen his body, why didn't you have them arrested for breaking the Roman seal? And why didn't you have the Romans torture the truth out of Jesus' followers about where the body was? After all if you could produce the body you could prove he didn't arise.

Caiaphas: I don't know.

Mr. Smith: You don't know? Come now, Caiaphas, that would have been the logical thing to do! Why didn't you do it?

Caiaphas: I don't know. Things were very confusing. The Roman guards hadn't seen these followers of Jesus at the tomb and the events at the tomb were hard to understand. I guess in the confusion, I didn't think about it.

Mr. Smith: Isn't the real reason that you knew it hadn't happened and that you yourself considered it possible that Jesus might have arisen?

Caiaphas: No! No! I knew Jesus couldn't have arisen because there is no life after death. The events, as reported by the Roman guard, were confusing, that's all!

Mr. Smith: Let me switch the questioning a bit, Caiaphas. On the afternoon Jesus was crucified was the veil in the Temple torn in two?

Caiaphas: Yes, it was.

Mr. Smith: Do you know how it happened?

Caiaphas: No, we investigated, but could not find out how it happened. We have a Temple guard posted outside the Holy of Holies beside the veil on a 24-hour basis, but the two guards on duty could not tell us how it happened. It just split in two at the end of the strange period of darkness, when we had the earthquake that Friday afternoon.

Mr. Smith: I have no further questions your honor:

Judge Noteworthy: Caiaphas, you are excused as a witness. Thank you for your testimony. Mr. Smith, you may call your second witness.

Mr. Smith: Thank you, your honor. I would like to call Mary of Bethany to the stand.

Mary of Bethany

Judge Noteworthy: Will the witness please face the clerk and raise your right hand.

Mrs. Jones: Do you swear to tell the truth, the whole truth, and nothing but the truth, so help you God?

Mary: I do.

Judge Noteworthy: Please take the stand and state your name for the record.

Mary: I am Mary of Bethany

Mr. Smith: Mary, the Bible has many Marys. I believe they are confusing to many people. Can you please explain how you fit in the story of Jesus?

Mary: Yes. I am not Mary the mother of Jesus, I am not Mary Magdalene, and I am not Mary the mother of James. I am Mary of Bethany the sister of Lazarus and the sister of Martha. My brother, sister, and I were good friends of Jesus.

Mr. Smith: Mary, tell us how you came to know Jesus of Nazareth.

Mary: It was through my brother Lazarus. Lazarus was always interested in religion. When a prophet began preaching in the wilderness, my brother went to hear him several times. This man's name was John the Baptist. Many thought he was the promised Messiah, but he denied it. Then one day he said that the Messiah was this man Jesus of Nazareth. Lazarus then began to follow Jesus. They became good friends and Jesus had a standing invitation to stay at our home when he was in the Jerusalem area. We live in Bethany, which is less than two miles southeast of the eastern gate of Jerusalem and on the route Jesus took when coming from Galilee. *(See Note 35)*

Mr. Smith: Your honor, we would like to introduce a map of Israel in 30 AD as peoples' exhibit #3 to show where Bethany was.

Judge Noteworthy: All right, we will mark this as peoples' #3.

Peoples' Exhibit #3

Israel in 30 AD

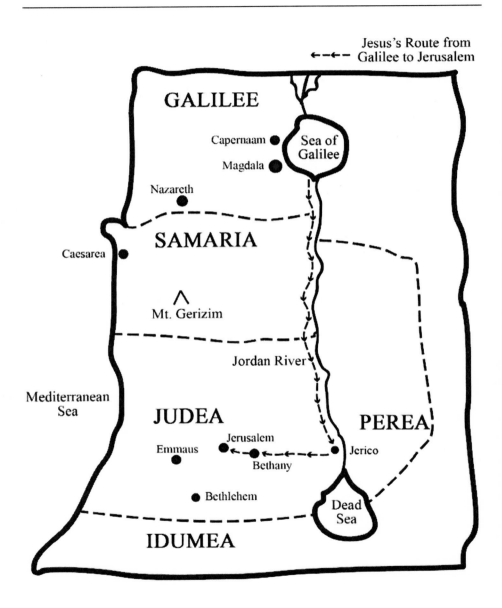

Mr. Smith: Mary, will you please point out Bethany and the route Jesus would take going to and from Galilee.

Mary: Yes, this is Jerusalem, here is Bethany, and this is the route to Galilee.

Mr. Smith: Thank you. Now, did Jesus stay with you often?

Mary: Yes, on several occasions he would stop by. He and my brother would often go up on the roof of our home on a hot Judean night and talk about religious matters until dawn. I would often just sit and listen. I have never heard such wisdom from anyone in my life.

Mr. Stockman: Your honor, I object, this is irrelevant and immaterial!

Mr. Smith: Your honor, this testimony is foundational to our position that Jesus was the Messiah.

Judge Noteworthy: I agree counsel. The objection is overruled. Please continue Mr. Smith.

Mr. Smith: Thank you, your honor. Mary, did you believe Jesus was the Messiah?

Mary: Not at first, I thought he was a great prophet, perhaps as great

65

as Elijah. But, later I became totally convinced Jesus was the Messiah.

Mr. Smith: What caused you to believe Jesus was actually the Messiah?

Mary: Three things convinced me beyond a shadow of a doubt. One was the raising of my brother Lazarus from the dead, the second was the resurrection and the third was the coming of the Holy Spirit at Pentecost.

Mr. Smith: Tell me about the raising of Lazarus. *(See Note 36)*

Mary: Well, Lazarus fell very ill and the doctor said he was afraid the illness was fatal. We had seen some of the healing miracles Jesus had performed, so we sent for him. He was about 20 miles away, at the time, over near the Jordan River. But Jesus did not come, at least at first, and Lazarus died. Four days after Lazarus died Jesus finally came. Martha and I told him how disappointed we were that he hadn't come sooner, since we knew he could have healed our brother. He told us to show him where Lazarus was buried. We took him to the tomb believing he just wanted to pay his respects. When we got there, he asked the friends with us to roll the stone away from the entrance to the tomb. Martha tried to stop them, saying that the body would have already started to decay and would present a strong odor. But Jesus told them to go ahead anyway.

Mr. Smith: Please tell us what happened next.

Mary: Jesus called for Lazarus to come out of the tomb.

Mr. Smith: And did he?

Mary: Yes, he came out still wrapped in his grave clothes. It was a miracle he could walk wrapped, as he was, with at least 80 lbs. of spices and aloes. But he did come forth and Jesus asked our friends to unwrap him. Lazarus was alive and well. I was never happier. I knew then Jesus had unusual power from God.

Mr. Smith: Did many people witness this miracle?

Mary: Oh, yes! A number of people were at our home grieving with Martha and I. They all went with us to the tomb and witnessed the miracle. They spread the word rapidly and I am afraid that was harmful to Jesus.

Mr. Smith: How could a miracle like that be harmful?

Mary: Well, as the word spread people started to follow Jesus in increasing numbers and I am afraid this rapid growth in followers caused the religious leaders in Jerusalem to see Jesus, as a threat to them, which needed to be removed. It was only a month or so after the raising of Lazarus that they arrested and crucified Jesus.

Mr. Smith: Were you there when they crucified Jesus?

Mary: Yes. Early that Friday morning Thomas, one of Jesus' disciples, awoke us about 12:30AM. He said the Temple Guards had just arrested Jesus. He was afraid they were going to put him on trial and try to arrest his followers. At first light Martha and I went to Jerusalem to see what we could find out. To our complete surprise we found out Jesus had already been tried by the Sanhedrin and condemned to death. We then joined a group of women from Galilee, including the mother of Jesus, who had come to Jerusalem for the Passover. We stayed with them through the horrible events of that dark day. *(See Note 37)*

Mr. Smith: Did Lazarus go with you?

Mary: No, it was too dangerous. It was known by many that Lazarus was a follower of Jesus. That, and the miracle of his rising from the dead, made him a marked man whom the religious leaders would like to have eliminated. So, my sister and I encouraged Lazarus to go into hiding, at least until we could see how things developed.

Mr. Smith: Tell us about the events surrounding the crucifixion.

Mary: Martha and I went with the women from Galilee to the crucifixion site and stayed there with the mother of Jesus until Jesus was removed from the cross and buried. John was also with us. *(See Note 38)*

Mr. Smith: Did anything strange happen that day?

Mary: Yes, several things. First, sometime after Jesus was nailed to the cross, a strange darkness fell over the land. It was like night had come 8 hours early. Then, when Jesus said, "It is finished" there was an earthquake, which was frightening, but at the same time the strange darkness lifted and we had daylight again. I heard the veil of the Temple had been torn in two and some people, who had died, came out of their graves and appeared to some of their former friends.

Mr. Stockman: Your honor, I object to this answer, it is unacceptable hearsay evidence.

Judge Noteworthy: I will sustain your objection, as to the dead appearing to people during this period. The balance of the answer will stand since the witness personally experienced them and these events have already been testified to and are in evidence based on the personal experience of others. Continue your examination Mr. Smith.

Mr. Smith: Thank you, your honor. Mary, did you see where Jesus was buried?

Mary: Yes, a man named Joseph of Arimathea and a friend of his named Nicodemus took and prepared the body for burial and placed it in a tomb about 100-yards or so from crucifixion hill. We wanted to see where he was buried, so we could come and pay our respects following the Sabbath observance, which began shortly after Jesus was placed in the tomb. *(See Note 39)*

Mr. Smith: And did you go to the tomb on the first day of the week?

Mary: Yes. And a most amazing thing happened?

Mr. Smith: What was that?

Mary: Well, we went just after first light to pay our respects and to place additional spices on the body of Christ. As we approached the tomb Mary Magdalene, who had left about 30 minutes or so before us, rushed up and said the tomb was empty and Jesus' body was gone! She said she was going to tell the disciples, and she rushed off. Not being sure what to make of it we continued on to the tomb. We found the stone rolled away, the tomb empty, and the grave clothes lying there, as if the body had vanished from within them Then an angel appeared to us and said that Jesus had arisen and that we should go and tell the apostles. So we started back into the city.

Mr. Smith: What happened next?

Mary: As we left the tomb, John came racing by us, followed a bit by Peter and Mary Magdalene.

Mr. Smith: What did you do next, Mary?

Mary: We started back to the city discussing these strange events. As we neared our lodging place it happened!

Mr. Smith: What happened, Mary?

Mary: Jesus appeared to us and said "all hail". I recognized his voice, but it was still hard to believe he was alive. He showed us his nail prints and the scar on his side. I was overcome with joy. Jesus asked us to tell the disciples what we had seen and to ask them to prepare to go to Galilee. We went into the city filled with joy. It was then I knew, beyond doubt, Jesus was the Messiah and the words he had spoken to me a week before were finally fully understood.

Mr. Smith: What words Mary?

Mary: About a week before this Jesus was having dinner with us in Bethany. I felt moved by his presence, so I took some very expensive oil and anointed Jesus' head and feet. Judas, who was there, berated me for it. He said I should have sold the oil and given the proceeds to the poor. But Jesus countered Judas by saying; I had done a good thing, because I was anointing his body for his burial. He said, "The poor you will have with you always, but me for only a little while." It only became fully clear to me after his crucifixion, what he meant by these words, and that he knew he was to be crucified. *(See Note 40)*

Mr. Smith: Mary, is it your testimony here today under oath, that Jesus of Nazareth raised your brother from the dead, predicted his own death, arose from the dead on the third day, and indeed, in your mind, is without question the Messiah?

Mary: Yes it is, without question it is so.

Mr. Smith: I have no further questions.

Judge Noteworthy: You may cross-examine Mr. Stockman.

Mr. Stockman: Thank you your honor. Mary, you are a very attractive young woman. Isn't it true you were in love with Jesus?

Mr. Smith: Your honor! I object to this question, it is irrelevant. Counsel should stick to the facts of the case.

Mr. Stockman: But, your honor, this question goes to the truthfulness of the testimony of this witness. I have a right to ask such a question.

Judge Noteworthy: I will overrule the objection, but be careful here counselor, if you go too far, I will stop this line of questioning.

Mr. Stockman: Thank you, your honor. You may answer the question, Mary, weren't you in love with him?

Mary: Yes, and my sister Martha was too, but it is not as you might think. I was not in a romantic relationship with Jesus. Everyone close to him loved him.

Mr. Stockman: You would have married him, if he had asked wouldn't you?

Judge Noteworthy: All right! Counsel, you have crossed the line! End this line of questioning.

Mr. Stockman: But, you honor, this questioning is essential to show the jury how biased this witness is.

Judge Noteworthy: Mr. Stockman, this jury is quite capable of judging the veracity of this witness. Now get on with your questioning on the facts of the case.

Mr. Stockman: Mary, regarding your brother Lazarus, isn't it true that your brother was not dead when he was placed in the tomb? And isn't it true that Jesus did not raise him from the dead, but that Lazarus revived in the coolness of the tomb and in fact never died at all?

Mary: That is totally false sir. A physician who was attending my brother pronounced him dead. He stopped breathing and his eyes were fixed. The doctor did not make a mistake.

Mr. Stockman: But he could have been wrong, couldn't he?

Mary: I do not believe so. In addition my brother was wrapped for burial with a napkin and wrappings about his head that would have made breathing impossible. He was in the tomb four days sir, no, he was dead and, if by some accident he was placed in the tomb alive, he certainly would have died in a short time.

Mr. Stockman: Mary let me question you about Jesus. When you went to the tomb on the first day of the week, were you sure you went to the right tomb? Couldn't you have made a mistake?

Mary: We went to the right place sir! We had seen the body of Jesus placed in this tomb on Friday. John, I, and some of the women from Galilee waited with Mary, the mother of Jesus, until he had been buried. We wanted to know where he was buried, so we could pay our respects later. Besides the tomb was only a 100 or so yards from crucifixion hill, you could see the tomb from that awful hill.

(See Note 41)

Mr. Stockman: Mary, when you say you saw this Jesus on the morning of the first day, you were in an emotional state, were you not? Hadn't you just found out the tomb was opened and the body was gone and didn't that have a profound emotional impact on you and the others?

Mary: Yes, it certainly did. I couldn't figure out all that had happened. Even though the angel told us he had risen, I wasn't sure that was true, because it is contrary to human understanding for that to happen.

Mr. Stockman: Isn't it possible Mary, that you, in that emotional state, just thought you saw Jesus? Wasn't it a case of your wanting to see him so bad that you had a hallucination? And just thought you saw Jesus?

Mary: Oh no sir, I did see him and so did the others. We couldn't all have been hallucinating at the same time! Besides I touched the nail prints in his hands, and we talked to him. No sir, that was real, Jesus was really there. He appeared to many others as well sir; we couldn't all have been seeing strange visions.

Mr. Stockman: I think you are wrong madam. No, I know you are wrong! People do not rise from the dead. It is not possible.

Mary: I agree, sir, people do not rise from the dead, but God can and in Jesus did!

Mr. Stockman: I have no further questions, your honor.

Judge Noteworthy: Mr. Stockman you may call your second witness.

Mr. Stockman: Your honor, I call to the stand Pontius Pilate.

Pilate

Judge Noteworthy: Governor, will you please face the clerk and raise your right hand?

Mrs. Jones: Do you swear to tell the truth, the whole truth, and nothing but the truth so help you God?

Pilate: By the gods, I do.

Judge Noteworthy: Please take the stand and state your name for the record.

Pilate: My name is Pontius Pilate.

Mr. Stockman: Good day Governor, we thank you for coming to testify.

Pilate: It's my pleasure. I hope I can be of some help.

Mr. Stockman: For the record will you please tell the court what position you held in 30AD?

Pilate: Yes, I was the Roman Procurator of Judea, Samaria, and

Idumea. I was the emperor's chief administrative officer or governor in that area. I served in this position from 26 to 37AD.

Mr. Stockman: And did you come to know a man named Jesus of Nazareth during that period?

Pilate: Yes, but I wish I hadn't, he brought me nothing but grief.

Mr. Stockman: Tell the court how you first came to hear of him.

Pilate: I'm not sure when it was, but I had heard some time before the events you are focusing on in this trial. I heard there was this itinerant preacher from Nazareth, who was performing some remarkable miracles; in fact he healed the servant of one of our centurions. I didn't pay much attention to him because all of his miracles seemed to be doing good, such as healing people, feeding people etc. I didn't see any problem in what he was doing. The country is filled with magicians and sorcerers claiming divine powers, he just seemed to be another one. I did learn at some point his name was Jesus of Nazareth. *(See Note 42)*

Mr. Stockman: Now Pilate, I understand that your headquarters was normally in Caesarea, but that at the Passover time you usually came to Jerusalem. Is that true?

Pilate: Yes, it is. The Passover was a major event and Jews came from all over the world to Jerusalem to celebrate. I went there because I could see many people on government business I wouldn't normally see. In addition, if there was any trouble, I wanted to be there. We also brought the Roman legion normally stationed in Caesarea to Jerusalem to help control the crowds and assist the legion stationed there permanently.

Mr. Stockman: So you were in Jerusalem at the Passover in 30AD?

Pilate: Yes, I was.

Mr. Stockman: How did Jesus come to your attention while you were there?

Pilate: I first heard from someone, that a few weeks before he had supposedly raised a man from the dead in a nearby town. I think it was Bethany. I was also notified that Jesus had been welcomed into the city on the first day of the Passover week by a large group of his followers. Some hailed him as their king.

Mr. Stockman: Weren't you concerned he was trying to foment a revolt against Rome?

Pilate: No, we pretty well knew who the troublemakers were among the Jews. The ones we were really concerned about were the Zealots. And none of them were followers of this Jesus. The people following him were religious people and either slaves or from modest and poor backgrounds. These aren't the types who foment revolt, and besides nothing this Jesus ever said, as far as I knew, even remotely encouraged people to revolt. Quite the opposite, in fact, he taught people to respect governmental authority and to pay their taxes to Caesar.

Mr. Stockman: When did you first find out the Temple Guard was going to arrest him?

Pilate: About 9:00 PM that Thursday night before Passover, Caiaphas came to my quarters before my wife and I retired. He said they were about to arrest this Jesus and that it was possible the Sanhedrin would impose a death penalty. He asked for some of my time the next morning to review the case. Only Rome has the power to impose the death penalty in Judea, so he needed my approval to carry such a sentence. *(See Note 43)*.

Mr. Stockman: And did you agree to give Caiaphas the time the next morning?

Pilate: Yes, I did.

Mr. Stockman: And did Caiaphas show up with the prisoner?

Pilate: Yes, about 8:00 AM there he was with this Jesus. He said he had been tried, convicted, and sentenced to death by the Sanhedrin for blasphemy. He also said they were afraid Jesus was plotting an armed revolt against Rome. I decided to question this Jesus, so I took him inside. Caiaphas and his followers couldn't come in because of some crazy religious rule they have, so I talked to Jesus without them.

Mr. Stockman: Did you find him guilty?

Pilate: No, I didn't. The charge of blasphemy means nothing to me. That is something attached to that strange religion of theirs. I was concerned about the charges regarding a revolt, however, the more I questioned Jesus the more convinced I was he was not plotting a revolt. His kingdom, he said, was of another world. I did find out through our discussion that he was a Galilean, however, and I decided to send him to Herod, who has authority in Galilee and who was in Jerusalem to celebrate the Passover.

Mr. Stockman: And did you send him?

Pilate: Yes, I did. Herod questioned him, and listened to the charges against Jesus leveled by the Sanhedrin.

Mr. Stockman: Did Herod find him guilty?

Pilate: No. He sent Jesus back to me saying he found no fault in him deserving a death sentence. Herod's soldiers evidently poked fun of Jesus' claims to be the King of the Jews. They dressed him in a purple robe, mocked him, and beat him, before sending him back to me.

Mr. Stockman: Is it clear to you that Herod did not see Jesus as a god or as the Jewish Messiah?

Pilate: Yes, that was abundantly clear.

Mr. Stockman: And after your conversations with Jesus did you believe him to be a god?

Pilate: No. He was an imposing individual and unusually calm in facing a death sentence, but no, I did not believe him to be a god at all.

Mr. Stockman: What did you do next?

Pilate: I tried one more time to avoid affirming the sentence of the Sanhedrin. I was convinced Jesus was innocent. Also my wife Claudia sent a message to me. She had a disturbing dream about Jesus; that he was innocent; and that I should have nothing to do with him. Claudia usually doesn't interfere in my official business. It was extreme for her to send me that kind of message. I remembered it was the custom at Passover to release a prisoner to the people as a gesture of goodwill and forgiveness. I decided to offer them a murderer named Barabbas, or Jesus. I was sure they would prefer Jesus because he had done nothing wrong, but I didn't allow for the cunning of Caiaphas. *(See Note 44)*

Mr. Stockman: What do you mean?

Pilate: I was told later by one of my centurions, that Caiaphas had packed the courtyard with his cronies, and that, when I offered the people Barabbas or Jesus, his people stirred the crowd up to ask for the murderer, while demanding the crucifixion of Jesus. *(See Note 45)*

Mr. Stockman: And did you affirm the conviction?

Pilate: I had to, after the crowd demanded Barabbas. I did tell them, however, Jesus was an innocent man. I asked for a basin of water and washed my hands in front of the people to symbolize the fact Jesus' death was not my responsibility. The crowd seemed to welcome this because they said they wanted Jesus' blood on them and on their children I don't ever remember seeing a more bloodthirsty group. *(See Note 46)*

Mr. Stockman: Caiaphas has testified he made three requests of you that weekend. One regarding a sign you placed over the head of Jesus, a request to hasten the deaths of those crucified, so they could be buried before the Sabbath began, and later for a seal and guard on the tomb. Was his testimony correct?

Pilate: On these issues it was. He really got hot about the sign; I had placed over the head of Jesus. I wasn't about to change it. In some ways I wish Jesus had been the King of the Jews. I believe I could have settled Rome's problems in Judea a lot easier with Jesus, than with Caiaphas and his cronies.

Mr. Stockman: Pilate, as you know, the body of Jesus disappeared from the tomb early on the first day of the week. Are you satisfied you know what happened there?

Pilate: Well, I had a long talk with Centurion Petronius, who commanded the legionnaires at the tomb. He told a strange tale, which I found hard to believe. But Petronius is one of our best commanders, so in the final analysis, I had to believe him. Beside Caiaphas told me he was totally satisfied with the performance of the legionnaires. He said he believed the followers of Jesus pulled off some magical stunt and stole his body. Since Caiaphas was satisfied and felt the matter was closed, I was happy to forget about it. I did hear that some of Jesus' followers were teaching that he arose from the grave and had appeared to many of them. I kind of half expected Caiaphas to try and convict some of them, as he had Jesus. I know he arrested some of them, but nothing further came of it, while I was there.

Mr. Stockman: Pilate, in summary of your testimony is it fair to say that you do not believe Jesus of Nazareth was a god, that to your knowledge he did not arise from the grave, and that he died as any other human being would have.

Pilate: Yes, this is my testimony.

Mr. Stockman: Thank you. I have no further questions. He's your witness counsel.

Mr. Smith: Thank you Mr. Stockman, and good day to you governor.

Pilate: Good day, sir.

Mr. Smith: Pilate, is it your testimony to this court that Jesus of Nazareth was an innocent man, and that you sent him to his death anyway?

Pilate: In my judgment Jesus was innocent of any violation of Roman law. He was put to death for a violation of Jewish religious law. His blood is on their hands not mine.

Mr. Smith: But you had to agree to execute Jesus, didn't you.

Pilate: Yes, but it was a mere formality. Caiaphas and the Sanhedrin requested it of me because they did not have the power to execute people. We had taken it away from them.

Mr. Smith: You could have stopped the execution couldn't you?

Pilate: Yes, but they wanted it carried out.

Mr. Smith: Isn't it true that Caiaphas blackmailed you into agreeing to the crucifixion?

Pilate: I wouldn't call it blackmail exactly, but he did put great pressure on me.

Mr. Smith: Please explain about this pressure.

Pilate: There were two incidents before the events in 30AD that set the stage. Not long after I arrived in Judea, I had a major problem with the Jews. I wanted to put a statue of the emperor Tiberius and some Roman symbols in Jerusalem to remind people who their ruler was. We routinely do this in all major cities in the empire. Caiaphas and the religious leaders went crazy over the idea. They said their religion prohibited graven images. They were so hot about it; some were willing to die to keep the statue and symbols out of the city. I finally gave in and returned the statue to Caesarea. A couple of years later I found it necessary to bring a new source of water into Jerusalem, so I decided to build a new aqueduct. I determined that, since it was for the people's benefit, they should pay for it, so I took the money out of the Corban, which is the Temple fund. The Sanhedrin and Caiaphas went emotional on me again. I couldn't reason with them. This led to some trouble and I had to kill some of their people before order was restored. They appealed my action all the way to Rome and the emperor Tiberius, and can you believe it, he supported the Jews! He told me I was wrong, and to please keep things quiet in Judea. I believe all Tiberius wanted was quiet in the conquered lands, and his taxes, of course. When the issue of Jesus came up and it looked like I was going to set Jesus free Caiaphas turned up the heat. *(See Note 47)*

Mr. Smith: How did he do this?

Pilate: Caiaphas let me know, if I did not affirm their sentence of Jesus, he would tell Tiberius, I had failed to take decisive action to stop a revolt against Rome. For good measure, he said he would tell the emperor this Jesus was saying he was a god and above Tiberius in importance in the Roman Empire. I sure didn't want Tiberius to have another complaint lodged against me, especially one like that. It was much easier to just give them what they wanted.

Mr. Smith: So, in spite of the innocence of Jesus and the warning from your wife, you agreed to the crucifixion of Jesus.

Pilate: As I said, it was their sentence, not mine. His blood is on their hands.

Mr. Smith: Sir, I'm afraid that washing your hands in public doesn't get rid of the guilt. By the way, in looking back on the matter, would you have done the same thing again, if you had the chance.

Pilate: No, the warnings of my wife came true.

Mr. Smith: How so sir?

Pilate: A few years after the episode with Jesus, I put down an uprising among the Samaritans. I took prisoners of some of their best men and killed them to set an example of what happens when people plot revolt against Rome. When Tiberius heard about what I had done and he removed me from my position. He called me back to Rome in dishonor. I was even exiled for my supposed wrong doings. To add to my problems Claudia, who seemed to be possessed by this Jesus, became a Christian and left me. I became despondent and finally took my own life. I committed suicide. *(See Note 48)*

Mr. Smith: I'm sorry to hear that. Did you trace your troubles to your treatment of Jesus?

Pilate: Many of them were linked to that situation. If I could do it over, I would not have affirmed that sentence.

Mr. Smith: Just a couple more questions, sir, and we will be finished. On the day Jesus died did you observe the darkness that fell on the land for three hours?

Pilate: Yes, it was very strange. Our scholars said it had nothing to do with an eclipse either, because it was the time of the full moon and you don't have an eclipse at that time.

In addition an eclipse of the sun only lasts 7 to 8 minutes at the longest. This darkness lasted nearly three hours. Some people associated the darkness with the death of Jesus. I personally didn't know what to think. *(See Note 49)*

Mr. Smith: We also have testimony that there was an earthquake, that the veil of the Temple was torn, and that some dead people arose and appeared to friends that afternoon. Can you confirm any of this?

Pilate: Yes, there was an earthquake about 3:00PM. It was not a major one. Regarding the Temple veil, I asked Caiaphas about that and he confirmed it happened. He said it was strange, and that it happened while two Temple guards were standing there. Maybe the earthquake caused it. I don't know how it happened. As to the dead people appearing, I heard rumors of it, but I do not believe it happened. Things like that just do not occur.

Mr. Smith: Regarding Jesus, do you believe he died on the cross?

Pilate: Yes, there's no question in my mind. When Joseph of Arimathea came and requested the body of Jesus, I sent for the centurion, who oversaw the crucifixion. He assured me Jesus was dead. One thing we Romans know how to do is to execute our enemies. Yes, there is no question Jesus was dead.

Mr. Smith: And my last question sir. Are you convinced you know what happened at the tomb and to the body of Jesus?

Pilate: No, it is a mystery to me. As I have testified, I believe the Centurion Petronius was telling me the truth about the events at the tomb, but they can't be explained logically. I am sure even Caiaphas doesn't believe the story about the body being stolen. If he had, he would have searched for it or questioned Jesus' followers about where they had taken it. Caiaphas might even have requested that we Romans question some of Jesus' followers. We have ways of making people talk you know, we have a reputation for it. Caiaphas did none of these things, which makes me believe, he did not believe the body was stolen.

Mr. Smith: Thank you for your testimony. I have no further questions.

Judge Noteworthy: Mr. Smith you may call your third witness.

Mr. Smith: Thank you your honor. I call to the stand Joseph of Arimathea.

Joseph of Arimathea

Judge Noteworthy: Will the witness please face the court clerk and raise your right hand?

Mrs. Jones: Do you swear to tell the truth, the whole truth, and nothing but the truth, so help you God?

Joseph: I do.

Judge Noteworthy: Please be seated and state your name for the record.

Joseph: I am Joseph of Arimathea.

Mr. Smith: Good day Joseph. Thank you for coming to testify. Would you please tell the court what your position was in 30AD?

Joseph: I was a Jewish rabbi in Jerusalem. I was also a member of the Sanhedrin, the Jewish High Council.

Mr. Smith: Were you a Sadducee or a Pharisee?

Joseph: I was a Pharisee.

Mr. Smith: As a member of the Sanhedrin, were you present at the midnight trial of Jesus of Nazareth?

Joseph: No, I was not.

Mr. Smith: Why were you not there, were you one of those Caiaphas said was out of the city? *(See Note 50)*

Joseph: I was never notified of the late night meeting. Neither was my friend Nicodemus. And no one was out of the city! At Passover people come from all over to Jerusalem to celebrate this feast. No good Jew would leave the city at that time. I believe Caiaphas knew Nicodemus and I would have spoken in defense of Jesus, and conveniently forgot to notify us of the meeting.

Mr. Stockman: Your honor, I object. This is speculation.

Judge Noteworthy: The objection is sustained. The jury will disregard the witness' imputing of motives to the High Priest. Continue, Mr. Smith.

Mr. Smith: Did you ask Caiaphas why you were not notified of the meeting?

Joseph: He said there was some miscommunication between him and his priests. He said he thought they had notified us, when in fact they hadn't. He blamed it on a bureaucratic mix-up.

Mr. Smith: Do you believe him?

Joseph: No, I believe he lied. We had previous discussions about this Jesus before the Sanhedrin. It was clear some of us felt he was not the threat to our faith that Caiaphas did. He wanted to get rid of Jesus. This became almost an uncontrollable rage after Jesus threw the moneychangers out of the Temple courtyard. This hit Caiaphas in the pocketbook and made him furious. I believe Caiaphas conspired to arrest, try, and convict Jesus before anyone could stop him. Part of that plot was to keep Nicodemus and me from the critical meeting where the Sanhedrin, under the strong influence of Caiaphas and his, father-in-law Annas, could convict Jesus.

Mr. Stockman: Your honor, I object again. This is speculation of the worst kind.

Judge Noteworthy: I sustain the objection regarding the motives of Caiaphas and the witness not being informed of the meeting. The remainder of the answer will stand, as an informed opinion of the witness based on behavior he observed. Please continue Mr. Smith.

Mr. Smith: Then you weren't notified of the 7:30AM meeting of the

Sanhedrin either?

Joseph: That is correct. Nicodemus and I did not find out what had happened until Jesus was before Pilate.

Mr. Smith: Do you believe Jesus was convicted legally?

Joseph: No, he was not. Two witnesses could not be found who agreed on any offense he committed. The judge has no authority to question a witness, and a capital offense trial cannot be held at night. In addition the High Priest must fast for 24 hours before confirming a death sentence. None of this was done. I felt so strongly about it that I forced Caiaphas to defend his actions at a later meeting of the Sanhedrin. *(See Note 51)*

Mr. Smith: And did he defend himself?

Joseph: He gave excuses and said my complaints were "technicalities." Since the majority of the Sanhedrin had voted with him, nothing came of my protest. *(See Note 50)*

Mr. Smith: Is it true that you asked for the body of Jesus after the crucifixion?

Joseph: Yes, It happened that I recently had a new tomb carved out of a hillside not far from the site of the crucifixion. I'm getting along in years and I wanted a burial place near Jerusalem for my family and myself. *(See Note 52)*

Mr. Smith: Tell us what happened on the day Jesus was crucified.

Joseph: When Nicodemus and I found out what was happening that morning, we tried to think of what we could do to prevent this miscarriage of justice. Unfortunately the process was too far advanced for us to stop. The only thing we could do was offer our respect to Jesus by caring for his body. So, I went to Pilate and asked for permission to bury Jesus. He sent for a centurion to make sure Jesus was dead, and when he satisfied himself he was, he gave us an order to the legionnaires to release the body to Nicodemus and I.

Mr. Smith: So you took the body and prepared it for burial?

Joseph: Yes, Nicodemus and I and some of my servants prepared the body.

Mr. Smith: Joseph, could you briefly describe, for the jury, how bodies were prepared in your time for burial? *(See Note 53)*

Joseph: Yes, our first procedure was to wash the body, and to particularly cleanse any wounds the body might have. Then we take a linen sheet or shroud about 16' long and 4' wide and lay the body on the lower half, folding the other half down to completely cover the body. Next we take a linen napkin and wrap it around the head. Once the body is completely wrapped in this way, we take linen strips about 10 to 12 inches wide and we wrap the body from head to toe with these strips. As we wrap the body, we place spices and aloes within the wraps. The aloes are in the form of a kind of paste, which we spread between the folds of linen. The spices and aloes form a kind of preservative, which slows bodily decay and offsets the odors of decay. We typically use 70 to 100 pounds of spices and aloes on an adult body. We used 100 pounds on the body of Jesus. When we are finished, we have the body encased in what might be considered a soft cast, as you might think of it. *(See Note 54)*

Mr. Smith: Thank you for that description. Joseph, this may sound like a strange question, but it is a critical one. Are you sure Jesus was dead?

Joseph: Yes, there is no question in my mind. His eyes were fixed, his color was pale, there was no breathing, and I don't see how anyone could survive the wound in his side.

The wound was not bleeding, when we prepared the body and the blood we did see was almost black. No, I am certain he was dead. Plus the Romans said he was dead and they know a good deal about killing people.

Mr. Smith: After preparing the body what did you do?

Joseph: We placed the body in my family's tomb, which was about 100 yards away from crucifixion hill. We then rolled a large stone over the entrance to the tomb.

Mr. Smith: How large was the stone?

Joseph: It was large! It was about 5 feet high and about 4 feet across. It took 4 of us to move it into place.

Mr. Smith: Did anyone watch while you prepared the body and placed it in the tomb?

Joseph: Yes, the mother of Jesus was there with a group of her friends and a disciple of Jesus named John.

Mr. Smith: Now Joseph regarding the day of the crucifixion did anything unusual happen?

Joseph: Yes, several things. First, we had this strange darkness for about three hours, which ended when we had an earthquake. The veil of the Temple, which covers the entrance to the Holy of Holies, was split in two as well. But even stranger, I have had two friends swear to me that on that day former friends who had died years before visited them. One had been dead 10 years and I believe the other one had been gone 4 years. I questioned them carefully about this, but neither one would back up even an inch from their stories.

Mr. Smith: When did you find out the body of Jesus was no longer in your tomb?

Joseph: On the second day of the week around noon someone told me the rumor was spreading about the city that Jesus had arisen. I immediately went to the tomb to see for myself. The stone had been rolled aside and the body was gone. But the grave clothes were lying on the ledge, where we had placed the body. I don't see how any body could have gotten the body out of the wrappings. The wrappings were tightly wound, and as I testified before the aloes cause the linen strips to adhere to each other.

Mr. Smith: Joseph after all of these events, what did you think about this Jesus of Nazareth?

Joseph: At that point I didn't know what to believe. Nicodemus and I had many conversations about him. We both had spoken to Jesus. Nicodemus went to him one night and spent a lengthy period discussing religious issues. We were convinced he was no ordinary rabbi. He had wisdom well beyond his years and he gave us insights into biblical truths that were profound. We were both convinced, he was a good

99

man, and probably a prophet sent from God, but at that point we did not see him as the Messiah. *(See Note 54)*

Mr. Smith: Joseph were you at the meeting of the Sanhedrin a month or two later, after Peter and John had been arrested and the Sanhedrin was trying to decide what to do with them?

Joseph: Yes, I was. Caiaphas was upset at their preaching. He warned them they would be in trouble, if they kept telling people Jesus had risen from the dead. They wouldn't stop, so he had them arrested. He wanted the Sanhedrin to sentence them to death, as they had Jesus.

Mr. Smith: It's clear from history Caiaphas did not succeed. What happened?

Joseph: That was interesting. Gamaliel, probably the most respected man on the Sanhedrin, got up and said something that was not only profound, but it stopped Caiaphas dead in his tracks.

Mr. Smith: What did he say?

Joseph: He said that we should do nothing to Peter and John. He said that, if this Jesus was who he said he was, and truly was of God, there was nothing we could do about this movement. It would spread, and if we tried to stop it, we risked striving against God. On the other hand, he said; if Jesus was just another person claiming to be the Messiah, not an uncommon thing in our time, now that he was dead his movement would die off, as others had, when their leaders died. This wisdom carried the day. Gamaliel may have had some deep guilt feelings over the actions of the Sanhedrin in dealing with Jesus. At any rate, whether he did or not his reason carried the day. Peter and John were set free. *(See Note 55)*

Mr. Smith: Just one last question Joseph. Did you ever come to the point where you accepted Jesus as the Messiah? *(See Note 56)*

Joseph: Yes, after the events surrounding the crucifixion, I became close friends with Peter and James the brother of Jesus. They were grateful I had tended to the body of Jesus. I listened carefully to the disciples' accounts of seeing Jesus after the crucifixion. I came to believe that, as difficult as it was to believe, it actually happened. Later both Nicodemus and I received the Holy Spirit and became followers of Jesus. At this point there was no doubt at all in our minds that Jesus was who he said he was, namely Christ the Messiah.

Mr. Smith: I have no further questions. Thank you again for testifying Joseph.

Judge Noteworthy: Mr. Stockman you may cross-examine.

Mr. Stockman: Thank you your honor. Good day Joseph.

Joseph: Good day Mr. Stockman.

Mr. Stockman: Joseph isn't it true that Jesus or one of his followers made prior arrangements for you to get his body after he was crucified?

Joseph: No sir, that is not true. I did not know he would be crucified until mid morning on that Friday.

Mr. Stockman: Did Nicodemus have contact with Jesus' followers regarding disposal of his body?

Joseph: No, I am sure he did not. He said nothing to me about this matter.

Mr. Stockman: Joseph, are you a physician?

Joseph: No sir, I am a rabbi, a teacher.

Mr. Stockman: I see, so you are a religious teacher. Do you have any medical education?

Joseph: No, I do not.

Mr. Stockman: Then how, Joseph, can you be positive Jesus was dead when you put him in your tomb?

Joseph: Well, the Romans said he was dead; he wasn't breathing; his eyes were fixed; there was no pulse, he wasn't bleeding from his wounds, and because of all of this I believed he was dead.

Mr. Stockman: If Jesus had been given a drug that placed him in a comatose state or a swoon, as it was called in your day, could you have discerned that?

Joseph: Maybe not, but I am sure he wasn't in a swoon.

Mr. Stockman: Joseph, if the drug caused the breathing to be so shallow it could not be detected would you be 100% certain he was not dead?

Joseph: I can't honestly say 100% sure, since I am not a doctor, but for all the reasons I stated I do not believe that was the case.

Mr. Stockman: So, is it your testimony before this jury that you could not be 100% positive Jesus was dead when entombed?

Joseph: I guess I would have to say that, yes.

Mr. Stockman: Now Joseph isn't it true you had become a follower of this Jesus before the events of the Passover weekend?

Joseph: I wouldn't say I was a follower at that time. I was intrigued by his teachings and by the miracles he performed. I was also impressed that John the Baptist said he was the Messiah.

Mr. Stockman: Isn't it true Joseph that you were infatuated with this Jesus, and that fact has colored all your testimony here with a bias toward Jesus?

Joseph: My testimony has been truthful, sir! I would not testify falsely! Your insinuation is insulting!

Mr. Stockman: I believe it is true! I have no further questions of this witness.

Judge Noteworthy: Mr. Stockman please do not badger the witnesses! You may step down, Joseph. Mr. Stockman please call your next witness.

Mr. Stockman: Thank you, your honor. I call to the stand Centurion Longinus. *(See Note 57)*

Judge Noteworthy: Will the witness please face the court clerk and raise your right hand?

Mrs. Jones: Do you swear to tell the truth, the whole truth, and nothing but the truth, so help you God?

Longinus: I do.

Judge Noteworthy: Centurion will you please take the witness stand and state your full name for the record?

Longinus: My name is Cassius Longinus. I am a centurion in the Legis 12 Fulminata or in your language, the 12th Roman Legion, called the Thunderbolts. *(See Note 58)*

Mr. Stockman: Centurion, was your legion stationed in Jerusalem during the events of the Passover week in 30AD?

Longinus: Well, we were officially stationed in Caesarea; however, the legion was brought to Jerusalem to help control the crowds and discourages rebellion during the Jew's religious holiday.

Mr. Stockman: Centurion would you please tell the jury briefly how the Roman Legions were organized?

Longinus: Yes, I'd be happy to. I have a chart to show this.

Mr. Stockman: Your honor we would like to introduce this as defense exhibit #1.

Judge Noteworthy: O.K., your chart will be marked defense exhibit #1.

Defense Exhibit #1

Organization of the <u>Legis 12th Fulminate</u>
(The 12th Roman Legion - The Thunderbolts)

A Roman Legion would normally be made up of 5300 men (4800 fighting men plus support people*). The fighting elements were composed of:

Element	Consisted Of
Squad	8 Fighting Men
Century** (80 men)	10 Squads
Cohort (480 men)	6 Centuries
Legion (4800 men)	10 Cohorts

* Support people consisted of blacksmiths, cooks, teamsters, medical personnel and administrators. In the early days a Century had 100 men, however, in later times the Roman Army reduced that number to 80.

** Longnius and Petronius were each Centurions commanding a Century

Mr. Stockman: Please go ahead centurion.

Longinus: Our lowest level of organization is the contubernium, or as you know it, a squad of 8 men. Ten squads form a century of 80 men. We have recently reorganized our army. In the old Roman army a century had a 100 men, which is where the term century came from, as well as the name centurion, who is an officer commanding a century. A century is roughly comparable to a company in a modern army. Six centuries make up a cohort, or a battalion in modern terms. Ten cohorts form a legion, so a legion with full ranks would have about 4700 men fighting men. This would be a mixture of cavalry and foot soldiers. The first cohort in each legion had 100 fewer fighting men but they had the 600 administrative personnel needed by the legion. This made a total of about 5300 men in each legion.

Mr. Stockman: Thank you centurion. As I understand it then, you as a centurion commanded a century of approximately 80 men.

Longinus: That is correct, sir.

Mr. Stockman: What duty did your century have on the Friday of the Jewish Passover week in 30AD?

Longinus: We were assigned to assist the Procurator, Pontius Pilate.

Mr. Stockman: And did part of your assignment that day involve the crucifixion of three individuals?

Longinus: Yes, it did.

Mr. Stockman: Have you and your men crucified individuals in the past? *(See Note 59)*

Longinus: Oh yes, it is not an uncommon duty for a legionnaire, particularly in wartime and in occupied territories. You see crucifixion is a cruel punishment reserved for the enemies of Rome. It is forbidden to crucify a Roman citizen. We save crucifixion for our enemies, so they will fear the power of Rome.

Mr. Stockman: Centurion, how long does it take the average person to die when they are crucified?

Longinus: Well, it depends on the person and how fit and strong they are. It also depends on how badly they were scourged beforehand. Some go into shock and die within a few hours, others may take a day to finally die. In my experience I would say it takes 4 to 6 hours for most to die.

Mr. Stockman: Are all those who are crucified scourged?

Longinus: Yes, most are, it's rare for us to crucify a person without scourging them first.

Mr. Stockman: Please tell the jury what scourging is.

Longinus: Basically we whip a person on the back while they are in a bent over position. We use a whip made of several leather straps. Each strap has pieces of sharp metal or pottery imbedded in it, so when the full force is brought down on the back of a person it rips the skin open causing extreme pain and bleeding. Some people have been known to die from scourging alone.

Mr. Stockman: Were the prisoners scourged on that Passover Friday?

Longinus: Yes, they were.

Mr. Stockman: Are any drugs given to the prisoners before their crucifixion?

Longinus: Sometime they are given some wine with a drug, which dulls the senses some.

Mr. Stockman: Centurion, were the prisoners on that Passover Friday offered any wine with a drug before they were crucified? *(See Note 60)*

Longinus: Yes, they were.

Mr. Stockman: Did you personally see the drink prepared and/or did you test it in any way to see what it contained?

Longinus: No I did not. The drink was prepared by some of the women of the city who, for benevolent reasons, try to reduce the suffering. They told us what was in the drink and I believed them. Besides I really wasn't concerned. The poor devils were going to die anyway.

Mr. Stockman: How long did it take the prisoners to die on that Friday?

Longinus: Jesus of Nazareth died in about 3 hours, the other two took longer, in fact, we had to break their legs to hasten their deaths, because we had to have them down and buried before 6:00PM that night. It had something to do with the Jews and their Sabbath observance, I believe.

Mr. Stockman: And were they down and buried before 6:00PM?

Longinus: Yes, we buried the two thieves. A man came to us with an order from Pilate giving him permission to take the body of the third. He took this Jesus for burial.

Mr. Stockman: Centurion, would you say this Jesus died in a shorter time than is normally the case in a crucifixion?

Longinus: Yes, most take longer to die.

Mr. Stockman: Can you state with total certainty that Jesus was dead, when his body was turned over to the person with the order from Pilate?

Longinus: I am certain he was, though I'm not a doctor.

Mr. Stockman: Is there any possibility at all he wasn't. Can you state with 100% certainty that Jesus was dead.

Longinus: Maybe not 100%, but I'm sure he was.

Mr. Stockman: I have no further questions. He's your witness Mr. Smith.

Mr. Smith: Thank you counsel and good day centurion.

Longinus: Good day sir.

Mr. Smith: Centurion, did you have your full century with you when you crucified the three people on that Passover Friday?

Longinus: Yes, I did. There was quite a crowd that followed us to the crucifixion hill. I understood this Jesus was quite a popular man with many in the city. Later, after the prisoners had been on the cross for an hour or so, I saw there would be no trouble and the crowd dwindled, so I released most of the century and just left one squad at the site to finish up.

Mr. Smith: Did you stay with your men to the end?

Longinus: Yes I did, I wanted to make sure our assignment was completed without problems.

Mr. Smith: Do you have any idea why Jesus died before the other prisoners?

Longinus: Well, I can guess. I understand he had been up all night. I also know he had been beaten by Herod's soldiers before we scourged him. He also had a crown of thorns pressed down on his head, which caused considerable bleeding around the head and face. He was terribly fatigued. He wasn't even capable of dragging his cross the 1/2 mile to the crucifixion hill. About half way there he collapsed. A man came out of the crowd and offered to drag the cross the rest of the way. I permitted him to do so. *(See Note 61)*

Mr. Smith: So, it is your testimony that Jesus was in worse physical shape at that time than were the other two prisoners and that this could explain his death ahead of the others.

Longinus: Yes, that's a fair statement.

Mr. Smith: Centurion, Mr. Stockman asked you about a drink offered to the prisoners. Was that offered before they were nailed to the cross?

Longinus: Yes, the women offered it to them, as we were leaving the city.

Mr. Smith: Now centurion this is a critical question. Did you see Jesus of Nazareth drink this mixture of wine and drugs?

Longinus: No, as a matter of fact, I was amazed he refused it. The other two drank all they could get. I had to move the group along or they would have drunk themselves into a stupor.

Mr. Smith: So, it is your testimony Jesus did not drink the wine and drug?

Longinus: Yes, of this I am positive.

Mr. Smith: Did Jesus have anything at all to drink that afternoon?

Longinus: Yes, near his death Jesus said he was thirsty, so I ordered one of my legionnaires to fill a sponge with vinegar and put it on a reed so he could relieve his thirst.

Mr. Smith: Are you sure it was vinegar?

Longinus: Yes, I am sure. I had some myself earlier. You should know this vinegar, spoken of here, isn't the same as your cooking vinegar used in the 21st century. What we called vinegar was a fruit drink that had not yet matured into a wine. Some called it a poor wine, but it was really what you would call a fruit juice.

Mr. Smith: Centurion regarding whether Jesus actually died on the cross, how can you be sure he was dead?

Longinus: Jesus must have known his end had come because he said, "It is finished."
After he said that, we could no longer detect any breathing or signs of life. When we got the order to speed up the deaths, I thought Jesus was dead, so I ordered a legionnaire to pierce his side with a spear to see if he was.

Mr. Smith: How could you tell by doing this?

Longinus: Well, if a person is alive and blood is circulating in the body it has a bright red color. If the heart and lungs have stopped, the blood clots and becomes a very dark red, almost black. You also get a white fluid, almost like water, which forms in the body. When we pierced the side of Jesus, we got a flow of dark clotted blood and some of the clear watery fluid, which indicated to us he was dead. And, if he wasn't before, the spear, which went up under his ribs piercing the lung and perhaps the heart, certainly ended his life. *(See Note 62)*

Mr. Smith: Centurion, some people may try to make a case for the fact that Jesus was drugged on the cross and that he entered a comatose state, or a state of suspended animation, from which he was later revived, so he could appear to have risen from the dead. In your opinion could that have happened?

Longinus: In my judgment that could not have happened. Even if they had planned that, and substituted a drug for the vinegar, Jesus was nearly dead when he drank it and the spear in the side would have ended his life by itself.

Mr. Smith: Centurion did anything unusual occur that day?

Longinus: Yes it did! About the time we nailed Jesus to the cross a weird darkness fell over the land. We had to get some torches so we could see everything that was going on. We also had an earthquake at about the time Jesus said, "it is finished." I have never seen anything like it. I also heard the Temple veil was split in two. It certainly was a strange day.

Mr. Smith: Tradition has you becoming a Christian that day because of these events. Did you? *(See Note 63)*

Longinus: You could say that. When I saw the darkness, and felt the earthquake I was amazed. And when Jesus uttered his last words and died, suddenly it became light again. I knew then that these phenomena were related to the crucifixion of Jesus. I said that truly this must be the Son of God. Later I had several conversations with centurion Petronius, whose legionnaires were responsible for guarding the tomb. His century is also a part of the 12th Legion. When we compared all of the events surrounding the crucifixion and the tomb, we both agreed this Jesus was someone special to God. We found out he had said he was the Son of God and would die and rise on the third day. Based on what I saw and experienced, he was who he said he was. I determined then to find out more about this faith. Later I became a Christian and was happy to share with others, my faith and experiences on that Passover Friday.

Mr. Smith: Thank you for your honest testimony centurion. I have no more questions, your honor.

Judge Noteworthy: Mr. Smith you may call your next witness.

Mr. Smith: Your honor, I call to the stand Judas Thomas.

Judge Noteworthy: Will the witness please stand and face the court clerk and raise your right hand?

Mrs. Jones: Do you swear to tell the truth, the whole truth, and nothing but the truth, so help you God?

Thomas: I do.

Judge Noteworthy: Please have a seat and state your name for the record.

Thomas: My name is Judas Didymus Thomas.

Mr. Smith: Good day Thomas.

Thomas: Good day counsel.

Mr. Smith: Are you the Thomas, who history has labeled the greatest of doubters?

Thomas: I am afraid so, sir. If someone doubts something, they are often called a "doubting Thomas". *(See Note 64)*

Mr. Smith: Could you please tell the court how you gained this distinction?

Thomas: After Jesus arose from the grave he appeared to the disciples, when I was not there. I was still in hiding with friends near Bethany. Later the disciples told me of Jesus appearing to them. I said I didn't believe Jesus had arisen and would not until I could personally place my fingers in his nail prints to prove he was alive. Eight days later I was with the other disciples in a locked room, because we still feared arrest. Suddenly Jesus appeared out of nowhere. He looked right at me, and seemed to know of my doubts, because he walked straight to me and showed me the nail prints in his hands and the scar in his side. He invited me to touch the scars to prove it was him. I will never forget that experience and never doubted the resurrection again. Because at first I doubted Jesus had arisen, history has made me the king of all doubters.

Mr. Smith: Did you see Jesus again in his resurrected state?

Thomas: Yes, 4 times, including the last time when he finally ascended to heaven from the Mt. of Olives.

Mr. Smith: Thomas, how did you come to know Jesus in the first place?

Thomas: I had always been interested in religious matters, and one day I heard that John the Baptist had pointed to this Jesus and said he was the Messiah. At the first opportunity, I went to hear him. When I arrived Jesus was up on a mountain praying, so I waited with a group for him to come down. When he came down, he spoke to us. He displayed a wisdom I had never experienced before. Then, at the close, he looked at me right in the eyes and said, "Follow me!" I'll never forget that look and those words. Needless to say, I followed him and joined the other disciples he had chosen.

Mr. Smith: Thomas, did you believe Jesus was the Messiah?

Thomas: I can't say I was 100% sure before the resurrection. He implied he was the Messiah and I was amazed at his wisdom and believed everything he said, but still I had some doubt.

Mr. Smith: What caused you to stay with Jesus during the years of his ministry?

Thomas: Well, it wasn't the pay! Jesus lived very humbly, as we did too, in fact, sometimes we didn't know where our next meal was coming from. There were really three things about Jesus that drew me to him. One was just his presence. He had a charisma about him that drew people to him. When you were in his presence, you just knew he was different and special. Then there were the miracles. I saw Jesus do things that no one else could. He healed people, some blind or crippled from birth. He raised the dead, including his friend Lazarus, which caused the Sanhedrin to act against him. Thirdly, I followed him because of his wisdom and teaching. Never have I heard such wisdom, and Jesus spoke with a distinct authority. Even the Temple scholars were confounded! These things caused me to follow him before his death, but the resurrection and the outpouring of the Holy Spirit at Pentecost caused me to serve him till my death.

Mr. Smith: Tradition tells us after the resurrection you carried the Christian message to the East toward Persia and India. Is that true?

Thomas: Yes, it is. I preached the Christian message until the day I was executed in India by some religious fanatics trying to defend their heathen religion.

Mr. Smith: Thomas some people are saying you or some other followers of Jesus stole his body to make it seem he was alive, so you could win new converts to your religion. What do you say to that?

Thomas: It is a lie started by Caiaphas, because he could not otherwise explain an empty tomb. If we had taken a dead body, we would have known he was dead and not whom he said he was. The cornerstone of our faith would have been gone. Why would we go out and preach Jesus had risen at the risk of our lives, if it wasn't true? We certainly were not trying to profit from our endeavors in any earthly way.

Mr. Smith: Some may also say Jesus had not actually died but had been drugged and that, when you took the body, he was actually alive and revived later. How do you respond to that?

Thomas: If we had been able to pull that remarkable feat off, Jesus could not have appeared to over 500 people and us in perfect health with his wounds healed. Besides, if that had happened, we would have wanted to keep him alive and with us, as further proof he had risen from the dead. No, if this had happened there would have been a human body, which would have eventually died and the fact would have been known to many people.

Mr. Smith: Thomas were you or any of your friends ever questioned or tortured to tell the authorities who stole the body and where it had been taken?

Thomas: No, no one was ever questioned about this matter, even though they had some of us in prison, in fact, they arrested Peter and John not long after Pentecost. They never asked them about the empty tomb.

Mr. Smith: Thomas, on the night Jesus was arrested; you fled with the others didn't you?

Thomas: Yes, even though on an earlier occasion I had expressed a willingness to die with Jesus. When I was staring death in the face, and it became evident Jesus was not going to use his supernatural power to defend himself, I ran with the others. I went to Bethany to inform Lazarus and the others about Jesus' arrest and to warn them of the danger the High Priest might try to purge all of Jesus' followers.

Mr. Smith: Thomas, let me ask you a question I asked Peter. On the night Jesus was arrested you ran away out of fear, yet later you preached about a risen Jesus Christ though you knew you would likely be killed for doing so, as you were. What made the difference?

Thomas: The resurrection and the indwelling of the Holy Spirit, which came at Pentecost. After Pentecost, we had some of the power Jesus had. We could heal and cast out demons. There was absolutely no question then whose we were and where we would go, if we were killed. In fact, Jesus said we would be persecuted for his sake, so we knew what was coming. Every one of my brother disciples was executed for the sake of the gospel except our brother John, for whom God had a special mission.

Mr. Smith: Thank you for your testimony Thomas, I have no further questions. He's your witness counsel.

Mr. Stockman: Thank you Mr. Smith and good day Thomas.

Thomas: Good day sir.

Mr. Stockman: Thomas, isn't it true, that in the days you lived, there were many magicians and sorcerers practicing their craft? And weren't many of them doing wonderful acts, which people couldn't explain. And didn't these sorcerers say their acts proved they had power from God, just as Jesus said?

Thomas: That's true, but their acts didn't compare to the power Jesus had.

Mr. Stockman: Can you prove that sir?

Thomas: I believe I can. You see the magicians and sorcerers basically performed tricks or illusions, as you call them. They would make things disappear or seem to be something they were not. They did sleight of hand tricks. Some even pretended to heal people, but they were usually found to be pulling tricks of one kind or another. Not one of these people ever healed someone crippled or blind since birth, and none of them ever brought someone back from the dead as Jesus had on at least three occasions.

Mr. Stockman: You call that proof? You haven't convinced me.

Thomas: Maybe no one ever will convince you, but let me further illustrate what I am saying with an incident that occurred after Jesus ascended. After Pentecost we disciples were given some of the same power Jesus had. Perhaps the greatest sorcerer of our day was Simon Magus who lived in Samaria. When he saw the power that Philip, Peter, and others were exercising, he realized it was greater than his own and wanted it. He pretended to become a Christian at first to get it, and when that didn't work, he offered to buy the power. Isn't it clear, that if the greatest sorcerer of the day realized the power of the Holy Spirit was greater than his, and tried to buy it, this proves the case for the power Jesus exercised? *(See Note 65)*

Mr. Stockman: Your honor, I move the statement of the witness be stricken as non responsive and full of hearsay.

Judge Noteworthy: Mr. Stockman, you may be the only one in the courtroom who saw that statement as non responsive. There was hearsay evidence in the statement, but it was relevant, and within the rules we have agreed to for this trial. His full statement will be permitted into evidence.

Mr. Stockman: Thomas, let me shift to the supposed appearance of Jesus after the resurrection. Isn't it true you and the others had a strong psychological need to see and believe Jesus had arisen? Wouldn't your whole religious movement have collapsed, if he didn't appear, as he said?

Thomas: What you say is true, but he did arise.

Mr. Stockman: Isn't it possible that you and the others had such a strong need to believe Jesus had arisen, your perceptions were effected by your emotions producing what you wanted to see rather than what you saw. We know people dying of thirst in the desert will see an oasis, which doesn't exist. Since the religious movement you tried to start would have collapsed, and all your work have been for nothing, didn't you have a strong emotional need to believe Jesus was alive?

Thomas: First, we weren't trying to start a new religious movement sir. Jesus simply wanted to correct some errors in the Jewish faith and fulfill the messianic prophecy. Regarding the psychological needs, I am not a psychologist, but I know what I saw. Jesus was no illusion or hallucination. I saw the nail prints in his hands and feet and the spear scar in his side. He talked and ate with us. I saw him at least 4 different times after the resurrection. If I was hallucinating, so were hundreds of others, and on one occasion 500 at once. No sir, Jesus was as real and alive after the resurrection, as anyone in this courtroom today.

Mr. Stockman: I think you're wrong, Thomas. People do not rise from the dead! I have no further questions of this witness.

Judge Noteworthy: Mr. Stockman, you may call your next witness.

Mr. Stockman: Thank you, your honor. I call Centurion Petronius to the stand.

Centurion Petronius

Judge Noteworthy: Will the witness please face the court clerk and raise your right hand?

Mrs. Jones: Do you swear to tell the truth, the whole truth, and nothing but the truth, so help you God?

Petronius: I do.

Judge Noteworthy: Will you please take the stand and give your name for the court record.

Petronius: My name is Marcus Gaius Petronius. I am a centurion in the 12th Roman Legion.

Mr. Stockman: Good day centurion, thank you for coming to testify.

Petronius: Good day sir, I'm glad to be here.

Mr. Stockman: I understand you are the centurion who commanded the detail of legionnaires, which was assigned to guard the tomb of Jesus of Nazareth. Is that true?

Petronius: Yes, it is.

Mr. Stockman: Will you please share with the Jury how that came about?

Petronius: Well, near mid-day on Saturday, during the Jewish Sabbath, I received an order to seal and guard a tomb of one of those crucified on Friday. I was told to place a guard on the tomb for a 48-hour period because there was a rumor someone was plotting to steal the body. I was also told a priest from the Temple would arrive shortly to show me where the tomb was located.

Mr. Stockman: And did the priest do so?

Petronius: Yes, about 1:00PM he showed up. I took my century of 80 men and we followed him to a tomb a short distance outside of the western wall of the city. I could show you where it was on the map, which is people's exhibit #1.

Mr. Stockman: Please do so, and also show us where the 12th Legion was camped.

Petronius: The tomb was located here, and our encampment was here about 3/4 of a mile away.

Mr. Stockman: Thank you. Now, when you arrived at the tomb was the stone over the opening of the tomb and to your best knowledge was the tomb undisturbed when you arrived?

Petronius: Yes, everything seemed to be in order.

Mr. Stockman: What did you do next?

Petronius: I had my men place the Roman seal on the tomb. I believe that process was described earlier in the trial.

Mr. Stockman: That is correct. And what did you do next?

Petronius: I analyzed the terrain and positioned my men for the mission. I decided to send half of the century back to our camp, with orders to remain on alert in case we needed them, since the tomb was close to our camp. They were ordered to report back to the tomb in 12 hours to relieve those on duty. I kept 40 men at the tomb including a squad of cavalry. We were only about 3/4 of a mile from our camp, so if trouble developed a horseman could bring reserves within minutes.

Mr. Stockman: Please tell us what happened that night.

Petronius: It was about 5:00 PM before I had all my men correctly positioned and we had sealed the tomb. Everything went fine for the first 11 hours of our watch and then it happened!

Mr. Stockman: What happened?

Petronius: About 4:00AM on that first day of the week a bright light appeared over the tomb and my men and I were frozen in our places. We could not move it was as if we had become frozen observers of what was happening at the tomb. There was also a rolling of the ground under our feet. It was the strangest experience I have ever had. We saw one man come out of the light, break the seal on the tomb, and roll the stone away. Then we saw a figure walk out of the tomb. He was bathed in light and seemed to be moving like a spirit more than like a man--kind of gliding rather than walking. *(See Note 66)*

Mr. Stockman: How long did all of this last?

Petronius: I would guess about 15 to 20 minutes.

Mr. Stockman: What did you do next?

Petronius: When we could move again, we discussed what had happened and examined the broken seal and stone. We looked in the tomb and found the body was gone. I decided then, I had better notify the High Priest, since he was the one who had asked for the tomb to be guarded.

Mr. Stockman: And did you notify him?

Petronius: Yes, we went to his house and a servant woke him up to talk to us.

Mr. Stockman: What happened next?

Petronius: He said he was sure the followers of Jesus had pulled some mystical trick on us and took the body. He told us to tell anyone who asked, the followers of Jesus had stolen the body while we slept. I told him we would be in trouble with our superiors, if we told them we were sleeping on duty. The penalty for doing this in the army is death. He said we should not worry about it, and that he would cover for us with Pilate. He gave us some money and told us to be sure we all told the same story. My men were happy to have the extra money and based on his agreement to cover for us with the Procurator, I agreed to his proposition.

Mr. Stockman: This next question is critical, Petronius, think carefully before you answer. Is it possible the followers of Jesus pulled some magical trick or illusion on you and your men, which threw you off just long enough for them to roll the stone away and steal the body?

Petronius: I guess that is possible. I have never had that kind of experience before or sense. But, I don't see how one man could have moved that huge stone.

Mr. Stockman: Let me be clear, your answer then is yes, isn't that correct.

Petronius: Yes, I guess so.

Mr. Stockman: Thank you, I have no further questions. He's your witness counsel.

Mr. Smith: Thank you, Mr. Stockman, and good day centurion.

Petronius: Good day sir.

Mr. Smith: Petronius, would you please tell the jury how you positioned your legionnaires around the tomb?

Petronius: Yes, I placed a squad of 8 men at the entrance to the tomb with orders to have two stands by the stone, one on each side, with the others to remain in the immediate area rotating the duty at the stone every 30 minutes. Another squad was posted in a perimeter position about 50 yards away in a circle about the tomb to warn us, if any one might be coming. I posted another squad on the hill above the tomb, which was an area from which a surprise attack could be launched. The 4th squad was held in reserve about 30 yards from the tomb. They were allowed to build a fire, lounge, and sleep, if they wished. I rotated the positions of the squads every two hours. *(See Note 67)*

Mr. Smith: Petronius, did any of your men on the perimeter that night report the approach of anyone?

Petronius: No, there was no evidence anyone approached through our perimeter.

Mr. Smith: Were any of your men engaged in any combat that night or were any of your men injured in any way?

Petronius: No.

Mr. Smith: Yet, your testimony is that one man broke the seal and moved the stone, is that not correct?

Petronius: That's correct, that's what I saw.

Mr. Smith: Where did this man come from?

Petronius: He seemed to come out of the light, which came from above us and settled over the tomb.

Mr. Smith: Was it a light like a torch or a fire would make?

Petronius: No, it was a soft white light. I couldn't determine the source of the light, but I remember I wasn't afraid at all, and my men reported they weren't either. The light had a soft calming quality about it. You could look at it and it didn't hurt the eyes at all. I have never seen a light like it before or sense.

Mr. Smith: In your judgment could one normal man have moved the stone in front of the tomb?

Petronius: No, I sincerely doubt it. It was a massive stone. It more likely would have taken 3 to 4 men to move it.

Mr. Smith: Was the man you saw walk out of the tomb Jesus of Nazareth?

Petronius: I don't know. I hadn't seen him before, but it must have been. They told us he was in there. And when we examined the tomb it was empty.

Mr. Smith: Petronius, breaking a Roman seal is a serious violation of Roman law isn't it? Doesn't it carry a death penalty for doing it?

Petronius: That is correct.

Mr. Smith: To your knowledge was there ever an investigation as to who did this? Was anyone ever arrested or tried on charges of breaking the seal?

Petronius: Not to my knowledge.

Mr. Smith: Petronius, you Romans have ways of making people talk that have information you want, do you not?

Petronius: Yes, we are well known for that. An army, as successful as ours, has to be effective in getting information from prisoners. *(See Note 68)*

Mr. Smith: Can you tell us then, why you or others didn't arrest some of the followers of Jesus and torture the truth out of them about who broke the seal and stole the body?

Petronius: No one I know of was ever ordered to do so, and to my knowledge Caiaphas never requested the Legion to do so. *(See Note 69)*

Mr. Smith: Just one question more. Petronius there are two possible explanations for what happened at the tomb. One is that Jesus' followers came and took the body of Jesus, while your men guarded the tomb, the other is that God intervened in the events, sent an angel to open the tomb, neutralized your soldiers so they could not interfere, and brought Jesus forth from the tomb alive. Which do you believe happened? *(See Note 71)*

Petronius: It is not common to human understanding for a person to rise from the dead, so I have a hard time believing God intervened, but I have to say it is the only explanation, which explains all of the strange events of that morning. Yes, I guess if I had to choose between the two alternatives you laid out, I would have to say God intervened in the events at the tomb.

Mr. Smith: Thank you centurion, I have no further questions.

Judge Noteworthy: Call your last witness, Mr. Smith.

Mr. Smith: Thank you, your honor. I call Mary Magdalene to the stand.

Mary Magdalene

Judge Noteworthy: Please raise your right hand and repeat the oath given to you by Mrs. Jones.

Mrs. Jones: Do you swear to tell the truth, the whole truth, and nothing but the truth, so help you God?

Mary Magdalene: I do.

Judge Noteworthy: Please be seated and state you name for the court record.

Mary Magdalene: I am Mary of Magdala, known more commonly as Mary Magdalene.

Mr. Smith: Where is the town of Magdala, Mary?

Mary Magdalene: It is located on the western shore of the Sea of Galilee, about 5 miles South of Capernaum and about 10 miles East of Nazareth.

Mr. Smith: So, you were in the area where a good part of Jesus' ministry took place?

Mary Magdalene: Yes, in our day most of the people in Galilee lived on or near the shore of the Sea of Galilee. When Jesus began his ministry, he often preached in the area and, of course, several of his disciples were from Capernaum.

Mr. Smith: How did you first come to know Jesus of Nazareth?

Mary Magdalene We heard that Jesus had performed a miracle at a wedding feast in Cana and that he had healed a nobleman's son in Capernaum. The next chance I had, I went to hear him, hoping I too could be cured.

Mr. Smith: Were you ill at the time?

Mary Magdalene: You could say that. Actually, since birth I had an affliction that seriously altered my life.

Mr. Smith: And what was that?

Mary Magdalene: I had frequent seizures, which caused me great difficulty physically and psychologically. These seizures were like your grand mal seizures, which are associated with epilepsy or brain damage in the 21st century. In our day the affliction was thought by many to be a sign evil spirits possessed a person.

Mr. Smith: Did you meet Jesus? Did he heal you? *(See Note 72)*

Mary Magdalene: Yes. One day we heard Jesus was in Capernaum, so I went to hear him, hoping I could be healed. After he spoke, he began touching people and healing them. I got close to him and finally he looked at me, smiled, and touched me. I'll never forget that look and that touch. Warmth flooded through my body, I had never experienced before or since, and I knew I was healed. I never had another seizure in my life. From that day on, I became one of Jesus' followers.

Mr. Smith: Did you believe from the beginning Jesus was the Messiah?

Mary Magdalene: I can't say I did, but it was evident from the beginning Jesus had special power from God and a wisdom that was beyond any man I had ever heard.

Mr. Smith: Did you come to the point where you did accept Jesus as the Messiah?

Mary Magdalene: Yes. I heard Jesus say he was the Messiah, and I believed him. He also said he would be killed and rise on the third day and he did. Any doubt I had before was totally removed, when that really happened.

Mr. Smith: Mary let me turn to the events of the Passover weekend. You were in Jerusalem with Jesus were you not?

Mary Magdalene: Yes, I was. I had accompanied Jesus' mother Mary and some other women from Galilee to Jerusalem with Jesus to celebrate the Passover.

Mr. Smith: Where did you stay?

Mary Magdalene: I stayed with some friends of Jesus in Bethany. Jesus and his mother stayed with Lazarus and his two sisters there.

Mr. Smith: When did you learn Jesus had been arrested?

Mary Magdalene: Early Friday morning word spread rapidly through Bethany that Jesus had been arrested. Thomas, who had been with Jesus when he was arrested, brought the news to us early that morning. He wanted to warn us of the danger that many of Jesus' followers might also be arrested including Lazarus.

Mr. Smith: What did you do next?

Mary Magdalene: That morning we women and the mother of Jesus set out for Jerusalem to see if we could see Jesus and find out what was happening.

Mr. Smith: And did you find him?

Mary Magdalene: We found out when we arrived that Jesus had already been tried and convicted by the Sanhedrin and that Pilate was considering affirming the death sentence. We joined a growing crowd outside Fort Antonia, where Jesus was being held. We were just outside the courtyard when Pilate came out and offered the people Jesus or Barabbas.

We heard the people; stirred up by the friends of Caiaphas, cry for the release of Barabbas and the crucifixion of Jesus. It was horrible and a terrible injustice.

Mr. Smith: Were you at the crucifixion?

Mary Magdalene: Yes. I didn't want to go but Jesus' mother Mary wanted to be with her son to the last, so the other women and I, along with John, went to that horrible place to be as close to Jesus as we could be in that terrible hour. We had some hope to the end, he would use his supernatural power to save himself, but he chose not to use it.

Mr. Smith: Did anything unusual happen?

Mary Magdalene: Oh, yes! There was a darkness that descended on the land sometime after Jesus was nailed to the cross. It lasted about three hours until the time we believe Jesus died. There was also a strong earthquake accompanied by thunder and lightning about the time Jesus died and the darkness lifted. I believe these were signs from God that he was displeased by what was happening to Jesus.

Mr. Stockman: Your honor, I object. This is pure speculation without basis in fact.

Judge Noteworthy: Sustained. The Jury will disregard the witness' last remark.

Mr. Smith: Mary, did you see them take the body of Jesus down from the cross and see him buried?

Mary Magdalene: Yes. Jesus' mother Mary wanted to see the body prepared and to know where he was to be buried. A Pharisee named Joseph asked for and received permission to bury Jesus. We watched as he and his servants prepared the body and placed it in a new tomb not far from crucifixion hill. We women also determined we would return after the Sabbath ended to anoint the body and pay our respects.

Mr. Smith: Did you observe the Sabbath, as you normally would?

Mary Magdalene: Yes, I did.

Mr. Smith: Tell me what happened when the Sabbath ended.

Mary Magdalene: Well, I couldn't sleep that night thinking of the terrible swift events that led to the crucifixion. I finally dressed and waited for the first light, which would end the Sabbath. As soon as I saw it, I told the other women with me, who were just getting up, I was going on ahead to the tomb and I would meet them there. So I gathered up some of the spices and aloes and headed for the tomb.

Mr. Smith: Mary, we have had testimony that there was a huge stone in front of the tomb, which took 3 or 4 men to move. How did you expect to move it?

Mary Magdalene: That's another reason I went before the others. I knew I would have to get some men to help us. Fortunately, the tomb is near a main road into Jerusalem. I knew at first light there would be many on that road coming into the city to do business. I planned to ask some of these travelers to help move the stone.

Mr. Smith: Did you get the help you needed?

Mary Magdalene: I didn't need it. When I got to the tomb I found the stone had been rolled away and Jesus' body was gone. I immediately ran into the city to tell Peter and John what had happened.

Mr. Smith: And did you find them?

Mary Magdalene: Yes, and they immediately began running to see for themselves. I followed them back to the tomb. Peter and John looked in the tomb and then went back to the city to inform the others of what had happened. Then the other women also arrived at the tomb and saw it was empty. As we were looking in the tomb and trying to figure out what happened, two angels appeared in the tomb. One said to us that Jesus had arisen, as he said he would and, to go and tell the disciples. Well, this frightened the women, and not knowing what to make of it, they started off for the city.

Mr. Smith: Did you go with them?

Mary Magdalene: No, I was so upset I just sat by the tomb crying and trying to figure what had happened. I was so upset I had not been able to pay my respects by anointing the body. *(See Note 73)*

Mr. Smith: Mary, are you saying that in spite of what the angel said to you, you were not sure of what happened?

Mary Magdalene: I must confess that's the truth. Nothing like this had ever happened to me before. All I knew was the body of Jesus was gone, and I couldn't pay my respect, as I very much wanted to do.

Mr. Smith: What happened next?

Mary Magdalene: As I sat there crying, a man appeared and asked me why I was crying. I couldn't see him well through my tears, but I assumed he was the gardener, so I asked him if he knew what had happened and where they had taken the body of Jesus. Then he said "Mary", I couldn't believe it, and I recognized the voice of Jesus!! I said, "Master" and I was filled with joy. He was alive! He then told me to go and tell the others he had arisen.

Mr. Smith: And did you tell them?

Mary Magdalene: Yes, I told everyone I could find. I found, by the time I got to Peter and the other women that Jesus had appeared to them as well. We were amazed by it all. We then recalled all of the words and signs Jesus had given us pointing to the fact this would happen. We tried, as best we could to reason through everything and decide what we should do next.

Mr. Smith: Did you ever see Jesus again?

Mary Magdalene: Yes, I was with a crowd of people in Galilee when Jesus appeared to us and proved his resurrection. It was a little bit like the old days when he preached and taught in Galilee. *(See Note 74)*

Mr. Smith: What happened to you after this, Mary?

Mary Magdalene: Well, I stayed close to the disciples and heard of

147

all the appearances of Jesus to them. They also told me Jesus was going to send a "spirit" to guide us. I was with the others at Pentecost and received the Holy Spirit along with the others. After that I dedicated my life to spreading the word of Jesus. I worked mainly assisting John with his ministry and helped care for Mary, Jesus' mother. Much of this was in Ephesus, where I was finally executed for my beliefs. *(See Note 75)*

Mr. Smith: Mary, let me see if I can summarize your testimony. Is it your testimony that Jesus of Nazareth healed you of severe seizures, that you observed him perform many miracles, that you came to accept him as the Messiah, that you heard him predict his crucifixion and resurrection, that you witnessed his crucifixion and resurrection, and that you taught these truths until you were yourself martyred for teaching them?

Mary Magdalene: Yes, this is my testimony!

Mr. Smith: I have no further questions; she's your witness counselor.

Mr. Stockman: Thank you. Good day, Mary.

Mary Magdalene: Good day, sir.

Mr. Stockman: Mary, isn't it true you were a prostitute before you met Jesus?

Mary Magdalene: No sir, I was not a prostitute before or after I met Jesus. I came from a merchant's family in Magdala. We were well off financially. I had no reason to become a prostitute.

Mr. Stockman: Wasn't Magdala know for its immorality and wasn't the town full of prostitutes?

Mary Magdalene: Yes, unfortunately there's some truth in what you say, but not every woman in Magdala was a prostitute, and I certainly was not one.

Mr. Stockman: Mary, you said you became a follower of Jesus after your supposed healing. Did you literally follow him around?

Mary Magdalene: Yes, whenever I could. I joined a group of women followers of Jesus. We would go with him on his trips to help him in any way we could. We would help prepare food, find water, and lodging, and do whatever else we could. I often spent my own funds to help with Jesus' ministry. By doing this, we could hear Jesus' teachings, observe the many miracles, and be a part of the ministry of this man of God.

Mr. Stockman: Isn't it true, Mary, you also took care of Jesus' sexual needs?

Mr. Smith: Your honor, I object! We've been down this road before. It is not relevant!

Mary Magdalene: I don't mind answering. The answer is, no!

Mr. Stockman: Isn't it true Mary that the group of women followers of Jesus was there to meet the physical needs of Jesus and his disciples, and that in fact, you all were prostitutes of a sort!

Mr. Smith: Your honor, I must protest again. This line of questions is irrelevant and immaterial.

Mr. Stockman: Your honor, you have allowed my opponents to bring in testimony attempting to prove Jesus was the Messiah. I believe I have the right to bring in testimony to prove Jesus was just a human man who sinned just like the rest of us.

Judge Noteworthy: You're right, Mr. Stockman. I will permit this line of questioning, but don't draw it out unnecessarily.

Mr. Stockman: Thank you, your honor. Now, Mary, please answer the question. Weren't you and the other women there to satisfy the pleasures of Jesus and his disciples?

Mary Magdalene: No, sir. Not in the sexual sense. I never saw Jesus even flirt with one of the women.

Mr. Stockman: Is that because he preferred men to women?

Mary Magdalene: No, not at all, sir! Adultery, sodomy, and fornication were all against our law. Jesus taught the law! He didn't break it! If he had done any of these things, his followers would have known he was a fraud and hypocrite. No, I never saw him sin. If he had broken the law, we would not have given our lives to his cause.

Mr. Stockman: But Jesus was a man wasn't he? Didn't he have needs like any other man?

Mary Magdalene: He certainly was a man, in every way. But he had a dedication to his mission and a discipline, I have never seen before. His sexual needs and other needs were simply subordinated to the higher purpose of his mission. He never married or considered marriage, as far as I know, because he was totally committed to God and his ministry, plus he knew he was going to die soon. He just didn't have time for a family. Any sexual activity outside of marriage was sin for Jesus. It would have compromised his ministry.

Mr. Stockman: How can you be so sure Jesus wasn't tempted and did not sin in the sexual area?

Mary Magdalene: I didn't say he wasn't tempted. I'm sure he was. What I said was, I never saw any indication of any sin in this area and I gave you reasons why he wouldn't commit sexual sin.

Mr. Stockman: So, you agree Jesus was tempted in this area?

Mary Magdalene: Yes, I'm sure he was, as all men are, but I don't believe it was a strong temptation. You see Jesus told us how, after John baptized him, he was led into the wilderness and was tempted by Satan. There were three major temptations and not one of them had anything to do with sex. I believe Satan is smart enough to know the areas where Jesus might have been vulnerable to temptation and sex wasn't one of them.

Mr. Stockman: Let me shift the focus here for a bit. Isn't it true Jesus was trying to start a new religion with himself as the head?

Mary Magdalene: No, that's not true. Jesus was trying to get the religious leaders to live in accordance with scripture not start a new religion. Jesus consistently preached in the synagogues and he preached and taught from our Holy Scriptures. He believed the Pharisees particularly had added so many rules and regulations to our law that it distorted the faith. No, Jesus lived humbly. He did not strive to be the head of a new religion. Actually the split between the Jewish faith and Christianity came long after Jesus died. *(See Note 76)*

Mr. Stockman: I have no further questions of this witness.

Judge Noteworthy: Mary, you are excused. Mr. Stockman, you may call your last witness.

Mr. Stockman: Your honor, I call Gamaliel to the stand.

Gamaliel

Judge Noteworthy: Good day, Rabbi, would you please face the court clerk and raise your right hand?

Mrs. Jones: Do you swear to tell the truth, the whole truth, and nothing but the truth, so help you God?

Gamaliel: I do.

Judge Noteworthy: Please be seated and state your name for the record.

Gamaliel: I am Gamaliel. Historically I am called "the Elder" because I was the first in a line of six Gamaliels who served as rabbis and teachers in Jerusalem.

Mr. Stockman: Good day, Gamaliel. Would you please tell us your position in 30AD?

Gamaliel: Yes, I was a doctor of Jewish law, a Pharisee, and member of the Sanhedrin at the Temple in Jerusalem.

Mr. Stockman: Is it true you were elected more than once as president of the Sanhedrin?

Gamaliel: That is true.

Mr. Stockman: And didn't you head a delegation from the Sanhedrin that went to Rome to present your grievances against Pilate before the emperor Tiberius.

Gamaliel: Yes, I did.

Mr. Stockman: Isn't it true you were perhaps the most respected leader of the Sanhedrin in 30AD?

Mr. Smith: Your honor, I object to this line of questioning. It's a waste of time!

Mr. Stockman: Your honor, I am just trying to show the jury how important this witness is and the respect in which his colleagues held him.

Judge Noteworthy: The objection is overruled, but get on with the direct testimony counselor.

Mr. Stockman: Isn't it true Gamaliel you were one of the most respected religious leaders in Israel in 30AD.

Gamaliel: Mr. Stockman, I appreciate the intent of your question, but it is not for me to judge how my colleagues perceived me. I can only say they honored me with several positions of responsibility, and I did my best to carry them out.

Mr. Stockman: Thank you for your answer. I believe your modesty helps make my point! Now, Gamaliel, were you at the midnight trial of Jesus held at the home of Caiaphas?

Gamaliel: Yes, I was.

Mr. Stockman: Did you hear Jesus claim he was the "Son of God" thereby committing blasphemy?

Gamaliel: Yes, I did. I couldn't believe what I was hearing. He said it loud and clear.

Mr. Stockman: And blasphemy is an offense punishable under Jewish law by death, is it not?

Gamaliel: Yes, it is!

Mr. Stockman: Did you vote to put Jesus to death for this offense?

Gamaliel: Yes, I did. It was clear he was guilty.

Mr. Stockman: What did you personally think about this Jesus? Was he a threat to your faith and your nation, as Caiaphas has testified?

Gamaliel: He was certainly a threat to our faith with his distorted teachings about the law and our tradition. When he drove the money-changers out of the Temple courtyard he disrupted worship there causing great difficulty. Yes, he was a person who needed to be dealt with or we would have had greater difficulty later.

Mr. Stockman: Tell us how he disrupted worship when he drove out the merchants and moneychangers, and please explain for the jury the function of these people.

Gamaliel: As you may know, the Temple in Jerusalem is the center of the Jewish faith. We believe God is physically present there in the Holy of Holies. People come from all over the world to worship in the Temple. An important part of that worship is the sacrificing of animals on the Temple altar for the forgiveness of our sins. People coming from afar usually do not bring animals with them so they need to buy animals for their sacrifices. I should note here that the animals used for the sacrifices must be with out blemish, for only a perfect animal is acceptable to God as a sacrifice. We have merchants in the Temple courtyard who sell animals for sacrifice. These animals are inspected by our priests ahead of time and are approved for sacrifice.

Mr. Stockman: I see, so these merchants are really providing a service for those coming to the Temple to worship and atone for their sins.

Gamaliel: That is correct.

Mr. Stockman: What function do the moneychangers play?

Gamaliel: They change the common currencies people use in every day commerce into silver drachmas, so they can pay their Temple tax. You see every Jew 20 years of age or older must annually pay a Temple tax of 2 drachmas toward the upkeep of the Temple and for God's work carried on there. *(See Note 77)*

Mr. Stockman: And that tax must be paid in drachmas?

Gamaliel: Yes, you see these other currencies have graven images on them and they are unacceptable for use in paying tribute to God.

Mr. Stockman: So, Jesus disrupted the operations of the Temple, making it impossible for some people to participate in the ceremonies, when he drove the merchants and moneychangers out.

Gamaliel: Yes, and that was totally unacceptable.

Mr. Stockman: Did you also see Jesus as a threat to the Jewish nation because he was gathering a group of people together who were likely to revolt against Rome and bring down on you the wrath of Roman power?

Gamaliel: I am less clear about this, but many did welcome him into Jerusalem as their "king". There was always the danger these people might try to over throw the Roman occupation, which could have brought the might of Rome down on us. We had developed a pretty good working relationship with Rome and Tiberius. We didn't want to risk upsetting this relationship. Jesus and/or his followers could have done that. We didn't want to take the risk.

Mr. Stockman: Gamaliel, as a Pharisee, you believed in the coming of a Messiah, did you not?

Gamaliel: That is correct.

Mr. Stockman: Did you believe Jesus was this Messiah?

Gamaliel: No, I did not!

Mr. Stockman: We have had testimony that Jesus met all the prophecies regarding the coming of the Messiah? How do you respond to that?

Gamaliel: Some of it is sheer coincidence. Other prophecies Jesus could meet just by knowing about them and conforming to them. No, the Messiah we are looking for is going to come as a great king with unlimited power and glory and he is going to free us from our bondage restoring the glory of our past, as he rules as our king. This Jesus was little more than a poor itinerant preacher. He was no king at all! He couldn't be the Messiah!

Mr. Stockman: So, it is your testimony that Jesus was not the Messiah, that he committed blasphemy, a violation of Jewish law carrying the death penalty, and he represented a threat to the Jewish nation.

Gamaliel: That is correct.

Mr. Stockman: Thank you, I have no further questions.

Judge Noteworthy: You may cross-examine, Mr. Smith.

Mr. Smith: Thank you, your honor and good day, Gamaliel.

Gamaliel: Good day, sir.

Mr. Smith: As a highly respected religious leader, you obviously have a deep commitment to the truth, do you not?

Gamaliel: Yes, I do. Bearing false witness is a serious offense and a violation of the ninth commandment of God!

Mr. Smith: Does that mean, sir, we can be sure you will tell us the truth here in this court?

Mr. Stockman: Your honor, I object to this line of questioning. The witness has been sworn. Opposing counsel is trying to influence the jury with these ridiculous questions.

Judge Noteworthy: The objection is sustained. Get on with the questioning, counselor.

Mr. Smith: What I am asking, Gamaliel, is will you, in your testimony, tell us honestly, if events occurred that Passover weekend, which you do not understand or comprehend, as opposed to putting the best "spin" you can on events to serve the purpose of defending your crucifixion of Jesus of Nazareth?

Mr. Stockman: Your honor, I object again. Opposing counsel didn't hear your last ruling.

Judge Noteworthy: This objection is overruled. The witness may answer the question and then let's get on with it counselor.

Mr. Smith: Thank you, your honor. Gamaliel, you may answer the question.

Gamaliel: Sir, I am a man of God. I take telling the truth seriously. You may be assured I will tell you the truth and will not try, as you say, to "spin" my answers to fit some preconceived version of the truth.

Mr. Smith: Thank you, sir; I will take you at your word. Now, Gamaliel, where does the Sanhedrin normally meet?

Gamaliel: We have a meeting room off the court in the Temple.

Mr. Smith: And how many members does the Sanhedrin have.

Gamaliel: We have 70 members.

Mr. Smith: Do you normally hold meetings in the middle of the night?

Gamaliel: No, but we have had evening meetings before, particularly on important matters and emergencies.

Mr. Smith: Can you tell me why you held the trial of Jesus after midnight and in the home of Caiaphas rather than in your normal meeting hall?

Gamaliel: It was an emergency and the home of Caiaphas was more convenient. Besides the official verification of the verdict took place after dawn the next day in our meeting place.

Mr. Smith: Isn't it true, Gamaliel, that your law says before you can convict a person; you must have at least two witnesses who agree on the alleged offense? And, in fact, if you can't find two witnesses, you must release the prisoner?

Gamaliel: That is what our law calls for, that's true.

Mr. Smith: Then why wasn't Jesus released? You couldn't find two witnesses who agreed on any offense could you?

Gamaliel: No, we couldn't find two witnesses who agreed, but Jesus convicted himself before the whole Sanhedrin. We were all witnesses to his blasphemy.

Mr. Smith: But, didn't he do this in response to an illegal question from the High Priest? And, if Jesus was the Messiah, then he was telling the truth wasn't he?

Gamaliel: You are technically correct, but he wasn't the Messiah and

the High Priest's question was a minor procedural matter, over sha-
dowed by the fact it led us to getting the truth of the matter from Jesus.

Mr., Smith: Did you actually hear Jesus invoke the name of God and
say he was the Son of God?

Gamaliel: Well he actually agreed to such words in a question put to
him by Caiaphas.

Mr. Smith: So Jesus never himself in his own words uttered blasphemy as specifically defined in your law. Isn't that correct?

Gamaliel: That is technically correct but he agreed to the words in the
question of Caiaphas, which was good enough for us.

Mr. Smith: It's clear, sir, you convicted Jesus illegally. But let me
shift the questioning. Gamaliel, did you have any hard evidence Jesus
or any of his followers were planning a revolt against Rome?

Gamaliel: No, but I believed Caiaphas, who said this was a danger. I
also knew Jesus was gathering many followers and it stood to reason
some might have a revolt on their minds.

Mr. Smith: You certainly didn't have any evidence to convict him of
trying to start a revolt did you?

Gamaliel: No, but we didn't need it, as I have testified, we convicted him of blasphemy!

Mr. Smith: But blasphemy has no standing in Roman law, does it?

Gamaliel: No, it doesn't. We used the argument about the revolt to help persuade Pilate to affirm the verdict of the Sanhedrin on blasphemy.

Mr. Smith: Well, thank you for your honesty! You admit you used a charge against Jesus, for which you had no evidence, to get Pilate to crucify Jesus for a violation of religious law, which had no meaning to Rome!

Gamaliel: Basically, that's true, but it was justified because Rome, without justification, had taken away our power to execute prisoners.

Mr. Smith: Gamaliel, in case you do not recognize it, you just admitted you and the Sanhedrin "bore false witness" against Jesus before Pilate, in order to get him executed for, what you believed to be, a violation of your religious law.

Gamaliel: We did not bear false witness since what we said had some truth to it. We did what we had to do to save our faith and people.

Mr. Smith: Were all members of the Sanhedrin at the midnight trial and early morning meeting?

Gamaliel: No, several were missing at the midnight meeting. Fewer missed the early morning meeting. I don't know the numbers exactly, but we had a quorum at both meetings, so the verdict was legal.

Mr. Smith: Isn't it true you cannot have a trial or verdict in a capital trial at night; therefore, anything done in this regard was illegal.

Gamaliel: That's true. That is also why we had the meeting in the morning, so it would be legal.

Mr. Smith: Please be serious, sir. You held an illegal trial, affirmed it in the morning, and then went to Pilate and lied about Jesus to get him crucified. Are you proud of how you killed an innocent man?

Mr. Stockman: Your honor, I object, he's badgering the witness!

Judge Noteworthy: Sustained. Get on with it counselor.

Mr. Smith: Yes, your honor. Now Gamaliel, regarding the merchants and moneychangers in the Temple, you testified earlier about what they did. Isn't it true these people provided an important source of income to the Temple and to the Sanhedrin?

Gamaliel: Yes, that's true.

Mr. Smith: And isn't it true you took large commissions from the merchants and money changers, a cost which they in turn passed on to the people in very high prices. And, in effect, weren't you really extorting money from the people through these practices?

Mr. Stockman: Your honor, I object to the use of the word "extort", and, in fact, to this whole line of questioning. It's irrelevant.

Mr. Smith: Your honor, I will demonstrate that "extort" is the correct word to use here and that this line of questioning is important to clarify Jesus' action against the merchants and money changers, which, has been testified to, was a factor in the condemnation of Jesus.

Judge Noteworthy: The objection is over ruled. The witness may answer the question.

Gamaliel: We were not extorting money from people. We were providing necessary services so people could fulfill their obligations to God.

Mr. Smith: Isn't it true that the prices charged by the merchants in the Temple were far higher than those normally charged for these animals outside the Temple?

Gamaliel: That's true but these animals had been inspected by the priests and were without blemish. Beside the profits went for God's work.

Mr. Smith: Isn't it also true you took large commissions from the moneychangers for changing their currencies into silver drachmas?

Gamaliel: I don't agree they were large, but yes, we did take a commission.

Mr. Smith: Isn't it true, Gamaliel that Jesus, in driving the merchants and moneychangers out of the Temple, was protesting that you were literally robbing people with the exorbitant prices, and making the House of God a den of thieves.

Gamaliel: He may have felt that way, but it wasn't true. And, as I have testified, all the profits went for God's work.

Mr. Smith: Not all the profit sir! Didn't the merchants and money-changers make a profit too, and didn't you get complaints from people that both groups were often cheating them by raising their prices.

Gamaliel: You're right, they did make a profit and it's true we did get some complaints. But not many and I do not believe there were any problems with our system.

Mr. Smith: Sir, poor people coming into God's house to worship and offer their sacrifices were being ripped off by these merchants and moneychangers and you permitted it to happen!

Mr. Stockman: Your honor, I object to this false assertion!

Mr. Smith: Your honor, this is not a false assertion. My point is that Jesus had a valid reason for driving these thieves out of the Temple. He was acting correctly and justly.

Judge Noteworthy: Let's move on Mr. Smith, your comments here should be saved for your summation. Do you have further questions of this witness?

Mr. Smith: Yes, I do your honor. Gamaliel, on the day Jesus was crucified there were some strange events, were there not?

Gamaliel: To what do you have reference?

Mr. Smith: Wasn't there a strange darkness, an earthquake, a torn Temple veil, and rumors of dead people reappearing?

Gamaliel: Yes, these things happened.

Mr. Smith: Let me ask you about the Temple veil. I understand the veil was split from top to bottom about the time the earthquake occurred and the darkness lifted.

Gamaliel: That's true. That had never happened before.

Mr. Smith: Would you please describe the Temple veil to the jury? I believe the word veil might mislead some people, as to the size and complexion of it.

Gamaliel: The temple veil is a large tightly woven tapestry 80 feet high and 25 feet wide. It hung from the ceiling across the front of the Holy of Holies.

Mr. Smith: I understand it was guarded 24 hours a day by the Temple guard. Is that true?

Gamaliel: Yes. No one, except the High Priest once a year, was allowed to enter the Holy of Holies. We believed God was present there and that any unauthorized person entering would die, so we had a guard posted day and night.

Mr. Smith: Do you know how the veil came to be split in two?

Gamaliel: No, I confess it is a mystery. We interviewed the guards about it, but they didn't know how it happened. It must have been a lightning strike or an unexplained result of the earthquake. No human could have done it unseen by the guards.

Mr. Smith: How about the darkness?

Gamaliel: That's a mystery too. We know it wasn't an eclipse, but our wise men can't explain it. We have earthquakes now and then and I do not believe dead men came out of their graves that day.

Mr. Smith: O.K., you do admit the darkness and splitting of the veil were unusual unexplained events?

Gamaliel: Yes.

Mr. Smith: Gamaliel, in your judgment what happened to the body of Jesus?

Gamaliel: I'm not sure. Jesus' followers must have taken it somehow. I interviewed Petronius, the centurion at the tomb, and he told a story, which was hard to believe, but to repeat, I don't know what happened to Jesus' body.

Mr. Smith: Let me now shift the questioning a bit. Wasn't Saul of Tarsus a student of yours? *(See Note 78)*

Gamaliel: Yes, he was and one of my better students, as a matter of fact. He was very disciplined and an eager learner.

Mr. Smith: You must be aware then, that he had a remarkable experience on the road to Damascus, which caused him to turn from persecuting Jesus' followers to becoming one of them.

Gamaliel: Yes, I know that happened. They called him Paul after that.

Mr. Smith: Did you ever talk to Paul after he had that experience?

Gamaliel: Yes, we remained friends, as many teachers and pupils do, and when he came back to Jerusalem, we had some talks about what had happened to him and about this Jesus of Nazareth.

Mr. Smith: How do you explain Paul's experience and his claim he met Jesus?

Gamaliel: I can't explain it. It may be he had overwhelming guilt for persecuting Jesus' followers and somehow it led him into that experience. I must say he never wavered in the belief he had encountered a risen Jesus, and he channeled all his energy into preaching Jesus had arisen, until he was martyred in Rome, during Nero's persecution of the Christians.

Mr. Smith: There's one last issue I would like to explore with you and we will be done. I would like to explore your defense of Peter and John before the Sanhedrin. I understand you saved their lives with your defense of them. *(See Note 79)*

Gamaliel: I don't know if I saved their lives, but it seemed to me we did not need more deaths to end the movement of Jesus of Nazareth.

Mr. Smith: We have had testimony that some weeks after the crucifixion Peter and John were arrested and that some members of the Sanhedrin, including Caiaphas, wanted to kill them for boldly preaching Jesus had risen from the dead. Is that true?

Gamaliel: Yes, it is.

Mr. Smith: Would you please tell the jury what you told the Sanhedrin, which caused them to release Peter and John?

Gamaliel: I reminded them that in recent times we had had two other men who had led religious movements professing to be the promised Messiah. One man was named Theudas and the other Judas the Galilean. In both cases, when these men were killed, their movements quickly died out and we heard from them no more. I told the Sanhedrin that, if the movement of Jesus were like these, it too would soon die, since he was no longer around to lead it. But, I also said, if the movement Jesus led was truly of God, there was nothing we could do to stop it, and to resist it would be to risk striving against God. The Sanhedrin listened to me and accepted my logic. We had Peter and John flogged, warned them to stop preaching Jesus arose, and we released them.

Mr. Smith: You used sound logic, sir. You seem to accept the fact that Jesus' movement could have been from God. Did you believe that?

Gamaliel: No I didn't, but there is always the chance it could be. Jesus did perform miracles, and his teachings were those of a wise man, though I didn't agree with them. I did respect Nicodemus and Joseph of Arimathea, who did feel Jesus' teachings had validity. I also admit Jesus fulfilled many of the Biblical prophesies regarding the Messiah, but he did not meet our understanding of how the Messiah would come, as I have testified.

Mr. Smith: So, you did believe there was a chance Jesus could be who he said he was!

Gamaliel: I believed there was a very slight chance. A chance we didn't have to take since, if he wasn't of God, his movement would soon die, as the others had.

Mr. Smith: Are you aware that down through history there have been many strong attempts to wipe out the followers of Jesus, including a major persecution by the Roman Empire in your time?

Gamaliel: I am aware there have been attempts to stamp out this movement.

Mr. Smith: Are you aware that this movement of Jesus did not die out, as had the movements of Theudas and Judas the Galilean?

Gamaliel: That seems obvious. It is evident in my being called here to testify.

Mr. Smith: Let me then ask you the ultimate question. In 30AD you said the movement of Jesus would soon die, if it was not of God, and if it was of God there was nothing you or anyone else could do to stop it. We stand here 2000 years later with conclusive evidence that the movement survived countless attempts to kill it, and has survived stronger today than ever. Isn't this proof, using your own logic, that the movement of Jesus of Nazareth was truly of God?

Gamaliel: I still believe my logic was correct, and, yes, if it was, then Jesus' movement must have been of God.

Mr. Smith: Thank you for your honesty. One last question, Christian tradition has you becoming a Christian yourself. Did that happen?

Gamaliel: No, I confess, however, I came close. My discussions with Paul, after the crucifixion, and the unexplained events of that Passover weekend did have an impact on my thinking, but I could not give up the beliefs I had taught others for so many years.

Mr. Smith: Thank you, sir, for your testimony, and for the logic, which saved the lives of Peter and John and helped us prove our case here today. I believe you were used by God to help further his kingdom. I have no further questions, your honor. The people rest their case.

Judge Noteworthy: All right, we have now concluded all testimony and are ready to proceed to the summations. Mr. Stockman, according to agreement you will go first. You may begin your summation.

Summations

Stockman: Thank you, your honor. Members of the jury we appreciate your willingness to serve on this most unusual and important case. For your contribution of time and energy, we are grateful. I am certain you will come to a correct verdict, when you have considered all of the evidence.

I do not believe your task will be a difficult one, because the evidence is clear. You must simply base your judgment on your own experience. The opposition, in this case, would have you believe a series of events occurred on that Passover weekend in 30AD, which could not have happened. It's as simple as that! People simply do not rise from the dead. It is contrary to our experience and contrary to common sense, and remember you must vote for our position, if you have a "reasonable doubt" that the oppositions case is true.

My opponent has put five witnesses on the stand to try and prove to you this resurrection occurred. I would submit to you, if you look at each one, you will find each is deeply flawed. Take Peter for example, he admitted on the witness stand that he was a liar. He admitted that on the night Jesus was arrested he denied he knew him three times. Was he lying then or is he lying now? His tall tales about this Jesus do not ring true. He is a seriously flawed witness. And what about this Mary of Bethany? She was obviously in love with Jesus. I believe she was having an affair with him. Would she then tell the truth about him, if it would hurt his cause and memory? I think not. She is a seriously biased witness who should not be believed. Then there's Joseph of Arimathea. He admitted on the stand he could not be positive Jesus was dead, when he received his body. I believe he was part of what could be called "the Passover plot" to make it seem Jesus died, when he didn't. Joseph had much to gain from this successful plot because, as a Jewish religious leader, if this new religion had succeeded, he would have been one of its top leaders, even more important than he was already. Joseph too was a biased and flawed witness. And then there was Thomas the "doubter." He doubted Jesus had arisen and he was right to doubt it. You should doubt it too for nothing like my opponent has described could or did happen. And lastly, there was Mary Magdalene, another biased witness, who I believe was under the spell of Jesus and probably in love with him. This Jesus was quite a ladies' man. The two Marys who testified here were both under his spell and you should consider their biased testimony in that light.

My eminent opponent would have you believe miraculous events occurred in Jerusalem, things none of us have ever seen or experienced. I believe there are logical explanations for everything that happened.

Let me explain what really occurred.

Our contention is that there was a clever plot, by Jesus and some of his followers, to make it seem he had died and rose from the dead. This would allow them to convince a multitude of people Jesus was the promised Messiah. They could then set themselves up as the priests and rabbis of a new faith. They would become wealthy and respected replacing the current religious leaders in the eyes of most of the Jews.

The plot centered on having Jesus drugged just before or sometime after being nailed to the cross. He would then seem dead when, in fact, he was only in a trance or swoon. We believe they made arrangements in advance to have Joseph of Arimathea secure the body, revive Jesus, and then have Jesus show himself to his followers convincing them he was the Messiah.

We have testimony the men crucified that day were offered a drink of wine and a drug, and later Jesus admittedly drank a beverage from a sponge on a reed. I believe the centurion, who testified Jesus refused the first drink, was either wrong about that or wrong about what drink Jesus was given on the sponge. In short, there was opportunity to give Christ a drug. Joseph testified he did not have prior knowledge of the crucifixion, yet he was a member of the Sanhedrin. I believe he lied to this court about being in contact with Jesus and his followers about seeking the body, before that Friday.

We believe Jesus revived, after Joseph washed his body and wrapped it carefully in spices, which would have facilitated the healing. Joseph may not have even placed the body in the tomb, or may have removed it on the Jewish Sabbath. Jesus then appeared to some of his followers to convince them he had arisen. After, he pretended to disappear into heaven. Our contention is he probably had a set back from his wounds through infection or such and died. We further believe he was secretly buried by his followers, who then proceeded to establish what has come to be called the Christian religion, by preaching he had risen from the dead.

The miracles supposedly carried out by Jesus when alive, and by some of his followers after his death, are not unlike those performed by the many magicians and sorcerers of the day. They simply carried the art to a new level of proficiency and fooled more people.

Our modern science of psychology has provided information on psychogenic illnesses, which can be cured instantly under the right psychological conditions. We believe the healing miracles attributed to Jesus and his followers involved these psychogenic illnesses.

It was not uncommon in that day, and this, to have people claim they were the Messiah. People have delusions of grandeur. Mental institutions have individuals, who for lack of self-esteem, take on the identity of some great person. We believe Jesus was this type of personality. He fooled many into sincerely believing he was the Messiah, when he was not.

He and his followers performed some tricks and illusions, which fooled many, including the Roman soldiers at the tomb. They faked healings and even fooled people into believing Lazarus had risen from the dead, when he too, like Jesus, was put into the tomb alive and brought out later seeming to have risen from the dead. Lazarus did not die at all at that time.

Much of my opponent's case hinges on the contention that Jesus was the Messiah the Jews were looking for. We have presented two of the leading religious leaders of the time and both have testified that Jesus was not the Messiah. Caiaphas, the High Priest, and Gamaliel, the President of the Sanhedrin, both have testified that Jesus was not the Messiah, who was foretold in Holy Scriptures. The truth is Jesus was just an itinerant preacher who aspired to be the Messiah and dreamed up a complex plot to prove to people he was. The plot failed and he died, as we all do.

No, my friends Jesus was not the Son of God; he was not the Messiah; he was a very bright, very clever, and very deluded man who tried something no one else had ever attempted. We believe he failed and died a physical death, as we all do. He is in a grave somewhere my friends, not in heaven, as my colleague will try to convince you.

The fact that his followers went on to preach he had arisen, and to begin a major religion is an accident of history. Many people believed the lies his followers told because they had a need to believe. The Christian faith was accepted early on by slaves, by the poor, and by the uneducated people, who by nature are superstitious and easily led astray by those who have good sales skills.

One other point I need to make. Mr. Smith has made much of the fact that Jesus was convicted unfairly and even illegally. Members of the jury even if that is true, and we do not concede the point, it makes no difference at all regarding the matter of Jesus' resurrection. The issue in the trial is not whether Jesus was fairly convicted but whether he arose from the tomb after having been crucified. In short he did not.

Ladies and gentlemen of the jury, when you consider the evidence and consider your personal experience, understand that people do not rise from the dead. How often have you seen this happen? In short it does not happen and it cannot happen. All you need to determine is that there is *reasonable doubt* that Jesus arose. I am convinced you will see the truth of our position and, in effect, find more than *reasonable doubt* that there was a resurrection. A truthful verdict must find Jesus of Nazareth did not rise from the dead. Thank you.

Judge Noteworthy: Mr. Smith, you may present your concluding argument.

Smith: Thank you, your honor. Ladies and gentleman of the jury you have a critical role to play here and I too thank you for your willingness to serve on this panel.

My esteemed colleague has told you Jesus could not have arisen because that is contrary to your experience. I would agree this type of experience is contrary to what we know, but not at all contrary to what God knows. I believe, we would all admit God has power over life and death and over the forces of nature. The people contend, and will show, that Jesus was the Son of God and the Christ, and you must believe, as we do, that, if he was, then rising from the dead was very possible. What is impossible to us is common to God.

Our position rises or falls with who Jesus of Nazareth was. Who was this itinerant preacher from the small Galilean town of Nazareth whose total ministry on earth lasted no more than 3 years, yet impacted history, as no other has done? It would be impossible for a conniving Jesus, like my opponent just described to you in his summation, to impact history as he did and teach with such wisdom that he to this day amazes scholars with his teachings.

History shows he was unique among men. So much so, in fact, that we in the western world set our calendar based on the date of his birth. Many beyond the Christian faith hold Jesus in high esteem. Mohammed, the prophet, who wrote the Koran and founded the Moslem faith, believed Jesus was born of a virgin, performed countless miracles, went to heaven without dying, and was one of the greatest prophets who ever lived. *(See Note 80)* Jews accept Jesus as an important teacher and rabbi. The symbol of Jesus' death, the cross, is probably the most recognized and reproduced symbol in the history of man. That Jesus was an important historical figure is undisputed, but the real question is, is he the Son of God and the Messiah? Was he, in effect, who he said he was?

We presented scientific evidence that Jesus was the Messiah. As you will remember, this evidence comes from the Old Testament of the Bible. This revered book, completed some 400 years or so before Jesus was born, contains some 300 references to the coming Messiah and at least 61 specific prophecies regarding him. We took just 8 of those prophesies to illustrate the point about who Jesus was and is.

183

Here is our People's Exhibit #1. As you will recall, these are only 8 prophesies of 61, all of which Jesus fulfilled. Taking these 8, Professor of Statistics Peter Stoner calculates the chances of anyone fulfilling all 8 of these prophecies by chance are 1 in 10 to the 17th power or 1 in 100,000 trillions. A committee of the American Scientific Affiliation further verified his work.

Members of the jury, that makes it virtually impossible for anyone to fulfill those prophecies by chance, and makes it a certainty that Jesus was the Messiah, because he did fulfill them. If you increase the 8 to a larger number, which is the truth of the matter, the probabilities of it happening by chance, go so high we can't even grasp the numbers. Jesus fulfilled Old Testament prophecy and was indeed the Messiah!

Being the Messiah and Son of God, as he said he was, makes his resurrection not only possible, but the only logical explanation for all of the events, which occurred on that fateful weekend in 30AD. Without this truth, our opponents are left with numerous unanswered questions.

Ladies and gentlemen my opponent has failed to explain numerous things, which happened in 30AD. Let me list some of them!

1. What happened to the body of Jesus?
2. How could the body disappear without the grave clothes being unwrapped?
3. Who moved the stone?
4. How could such a huge stone be moved by one person?

5. How could an elite Roman Guard be fooled by some uneducated fearful followers of Jesus?

6. What caused the 3 hours of darkness?

7. How did the temple veil get split in two?

8. How could so many people report seeing Jesus alive, if he wasn't alive?

9. Why would 11 men, fearful before the resurrection, go to their deaths with courage, and preaching Jesus arose, if it did not happen?

These and other questions remain unanswered by my opponent. We gave you answers for every one. In our argument we explain everything that happened. They cannot! Our case explains everything that happened that fateful weekend in 30 AD. My opponent's case leaves numerous elements unexplained or illogically explained.

My colleague would have you believe that Jesus and his followers wanted to start a new religion, so they could become the leaders in order to gain wealth and power. Yet Jesus practiced frugality. There is no evidence at all that he or his followers tried to benefit materially or in any other way from their teaching. Eleven of the 12 disciples, who ran away afraid on the night Jesus was arrested, preached boldly after the crucifixion that Jesus had arisen. They preached this message with such courage that 11 of the 12 were executed for their conviction. What changed them? Why fear one day and unexplainable courage the next? I would submit to you the difference was they had seen the risen Christ in between. That made the difference! My opponent cannot explain this fact. And not one disciple died rich, quite the contrary, not one sought wealth or fame. The case of my opponent leaves too many unanswered questions for it to be the truth.

My opponent suggests Jesus was sexually permissive, yet presents no evidence to support this falsehood. For this to be true Jesus would have had to violate the very biblical teachings he died to preserve and he would have been seen a hypocrite to his followers.

No, Jesus was not sexually permissive. If he had been, his disciples would not have followed him to their deaths.

I would submit to you members of the jury that the testimony you heard in this case from our witnesses had the ring of truth to it. For example the first reaction of Jesus' followers, when they heard the tomb was empty was essentially, who took the body and where is it? The first reaction was not one of joy believing he had arisen, even though he said he would. I would submit to you their first reaction was human, the same as yours must be, namely people don't rise from the dead, so Jesus must still be dead. But they learned, what you must accept, that God has the power over life and death and Jesus did arise, as he said he would. And Thomas, bless his soul, his actions too were so human, they have the ring of truth to them as well. When he was told by those he knew and trusted, he still wouldn't believe Jesus had arisen. But he believed, when Jesus appeared to him and gave him proof positive he was alive. Thomas had his doubt removed. Thomas doubted so we could believe!

As I said at the beginning of our case, our argument, hinges on who Jesus really was. If he was the Son of God, then everything that we say happened is entirely possible. If he were just a man, and not God, then he would be bound by the laws of nature, as we are.

So this whole case turns on whom Jesus really was. You have to determine whether he was a delusional mental case, who lied about who he was and about the resurrection, or was he who he said he was and truly the Messiah and Son of God. Was Jesus a revolutionary plotting a revolt against Rome or was the loving son of sent from heaven preaching God's truth? The reasons for believing Jesus was the Messiah are many. I have sighted Old Testament prophecy, the impact of Jesus on history, His impact on the lives of men and women down through the ages. Then there is the purity and profoundness of his teachings, admired and followed by many even many non-Christians.

And then we have the testimony of Gamaliel, one of their witnesses, who I believe helped to prove our case. The words and logic of Gamaliel point to the truth of our position. As you will remember, Gamaliel in testifying before the Sanhedrin, in defense of Peter and John, said in essence, if Jesus was the Messiah and if the disciples spoke the truth, no one could stop the truth from spreading, because it was from God. He said if Jesus wasn't who he said he was, his movement would soon die as others had. History he said, in effect, will prove who Jesus really was!

Ladies and gentleman of the jury I submit Gamaliel was exactly right! History has proven Jesus was who he said he was. Kings and emperors throughout history have tried to stamp out the Christian message and they have all failed. The breadth and strength of Christianity today, and down through history, testify to the truth that this itinerant preacher from the nondescript town of Nazareth, who preached and taught for less than three years, has impacted history like no one before or since.

Could that have been accomplished by a delusional man who didn't know who he really was? To believe that would stretch credulity far beyond that needed to accept that the Son of God could rise from the dead. Many witnesses in this trial have said the things they saw were, "beyond human understanding", and they were, but they were not beyond God's understanding or power.

Ladies and gentlemen I close by showing you a "Mountain of Evidence", which proves our case conclusively.

People's Summation Exhibit #1
Mountain of Evidence

The Mountain Of Evidence Points To The Truth That:

Jesus Christ Arose!

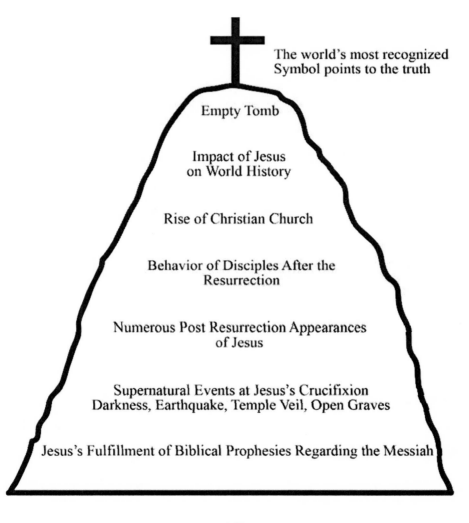

The world's most recognized
Symbol points to the truth

Empty Tomb

Impact of Jesus
on World History

Rise of Christian Church

Behavior of Disciples After the
Resurrection

Numerous Post Resurrection Appearances
of Jesus

Supernatural Events at Jesus's Crucifixion
Darkness, Earthquake, Temple Veil, Open Graves

Jesus's Fulfillment of Biblical Prophesies Regarding the Messiah

Here members of the jury are the main elements of evidence, which proves beyond reasonable doubt Jesus arose from the grave, as he said he would.

1. Jesus fulfilled the Biblical prophesies on the coming Messiah and was the Messiah
2. There were supernatural events at his crucifixion
3. Jesus made numerous post crucifixion appearances
4. Eleven of the twelve disciples went to their deaths because they preached Jesus arose
5. The Christian Church has arisen across the world in spite of attempts to kill it.
6. Jesus has impacted the world, as no other person in human history, yet he lived only 33 years and ministered for only 3 years.
7. The tomb was empty because Jesus had arisen.

Ladies and gentleman of the jury you have to decide where the truth lies. You must decide which position accounts for all of the facts presented in this trial. When you consider, which position presents you with the full picture and the finished puzzle, I am convinced you will decide this Jesus of Nazareth indeed was who he said he was. And indeed did what he said he would do, namely die for the sins of mankind and rise again on the third day. THE TOMB WAS EMPTY BECAUSE JESUS HAD ARISEN FROM THE DEAD.

Thank you for your attention and we look forward to your verdict.

Judge Noteworthy: Ladies and gentlemen of the jury you have before you a most interesting and unique case. Deciding it may be difficult. However, you must find for one side or the other "beyond a reasonable doubt".

One point of guidance I can give you when you consider the evidence presented here. Truth has a quality that falsehood does not have, and that is that all of the pieces or facts fit together.

I have seen this principle applied many times since I have been on this bench. The truthful side can explain all the facts, not just some of them. The truthful side does not leave unexplained facts.

The truth is like a finished jigsaw puzzle—all of the pieces fit together perfectly. No pieces are left over—no facts left unexplained.

You have heard the testimony of the witnesses on both sides of this case. Ask yourself which side has the "ring of truth" about it because it most effectively explains all of the facts presented in this case.

The burden of proof is beyond a reasonable doubt. Note please, that the standard is not just doubt, but reasonable doubt. The doubt must be supported by logic and reason to meet the standard of "reasonable doubt".

If you find the case presented by the people explains all of the facts and is reasonable and consistent, you must find that Jesus arose from the dead. If you are convinced beyond a reasonable doubt that the case presented by the defense is true, you must find Jesus did not arise from the dead, and that the story of the resurrection was a ruse and hoax perpetrated on history by the followers of Jesus.

Ladies and gentlemen the verdict is in your hands. I wish you well in your deliberations.

The jurors are dismissed to begin their deliberations.

Exhibit of Crucifixion Timeline

Timeline Of Events Surrounding
Jesus's Crucifixion
(Thursday Afternoon Through Easter Sunday)

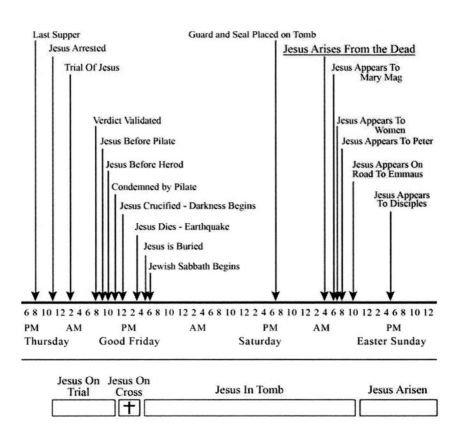

OFFICIAL JURY BALLOT
17TH CIRCUIT COURT
OF THE STATE OF MICHIGAN

I the undersigned do solemnly swear that I have served as a juror in the case of Jesus of Nazareth, that I have heard and considered all of the evidence in the case and I have reached the independent verdict checked below without outside interference or influence. The verdict is solely my own and has been independently determined.

Please check your verdict:

_____   **It is my judgment, beyond reasonable doubt, that Jesus of Nazareth physically arose from the grave in 30 AD.**

_____   **It is my judgment that I cannot say, beyond reasonable doubt, Jesus of Nazareth rose from the grave in 30 AD.**

_____   _____
Juror Signature   Date

Bibliography

1. Brandel, Fernando, *A History of Western Civilization,* (Translated by Richard Mayne), Penguin Books, New York, New York. 1995. PP-600.

2. *Encarta 95 Encyclopedia*, Microsoft Corporation, CD-ROM, 1994.

3. Goldberg, David, and Rayner, John, *The Jewish People - Their History and TheirReligion,* Viking, New York, New York. 1987. PP-402.

4. Gibbon, Edward, *The Decline and Fall of the Roman Empire,* (A one volume abridgment by DM Low), Harcourt Brace and Co., New York New York. 1960. PP-924.

5. Graham, Eleanor, *The Story of Jesus,* Puffin Books, London, England, (First published 1959, revised and reissued 1993). PP-206.

6. Grant, Michael, *The Army of the Caesars,* M. Evens and Co., New York, New York. 1974. PP-366.

7. Habermas, Gary, *The Historical Jesus. Ancient Evidence For The Life Of Christ,*College Press Publishing Co., Poplin, Missouri. 1966. PP-304.

8. Haley, Henry H., *Haley's Bible Handbook - 24th Edition,* Zondervan, Grand Rapids, Michigan. 1965. PP-860.

9. Joseph's, Flavius, *The Complete Writings of Josephus,* (WilliamWhiston,Translator), Kregel Publications, Grand Rapids, Michigan. 1981. PP-775.

Bibliography

10. Lockyear, Herbert, *All The Men Of The Bible,* Lamplighter Books (Zondervan), Grand Rapids, Michigan. 1958. PP- 374.

11. Mc Dowell, Josh, *Evidence That Demands A Verdict,* Campus Crusade For Christ, U.S.A. 1972. PP-378.

12. McIntosh and Twyman (Translators), *The Archko Volume or the Archeological Writings of the Sanhederim and the Talmud's of the Jews,* Keats Publishing Inc., New Caanan, Connecticut. 1975. PP- 248.

13. Morison, Frank, *Who Moved The Stone?,* Zondervan, Grand Rapids, Michigan. 1978. PP-193.

14. Robertson, A.T., *Harmony Of The Gospels,* Harper & Bros., N.Y., New York. 1922. PP-305.

15. Schonfield, Hugh J., *The Passover Plot,* Bernard Geis Assoc., (Distributed by Random House), N.Y., New York. 1965. PP-287.

16. Shakir, *M.H., (Translator), The Qur'an*, Taahrike Tarsile Qur'an Inc., Elmhurst, New York. Sixth Edition 1990. PP-432.

17. Spong, John Shelby, *Resurrection - Myth or Reality?* Harper, San Francisco, Calif. 1994. PP-320.

Notes and Biblical References

In thinking about the resurrection of Jesus of Nazareth it is critical for one to carefully examine the assumptions from which they start. For example, if one assumes, because it is not common to human experience, that it is not possible for anyone to rise from the dead after being entombed as long as Jesus was, then one starts from the premise it could not happen, because it is impossible. This is basically the starting point for Spong (17), and Schonfield (15). It is not surprising then, that they both come out at the end saying Jesus of Nazareth did not rise from the dead. If one starts with an open mind or the belief that there is a God with power over life and death, which could raise one from the dead, if he wished, then the resurrection story becomes a real possibility.

It is also important to make an assumption regarding who Jesus of Nazareth was. If he was just a clever con-man or just a good human being, then a resurrection is less likely to be a reality than if he was who he said he was, namely the Son of God.

A third assumption is also critical, and that relates to ones perception of the Bible as a conveyer of truth. If the Bible is the inerrant "Word of God", then certain truths follow logically, however, if the Bible is simply a human book from antiquity, filled with errors and contradictions, then it cannot be relied on to give much help in determining whether Jesus actually arose or not.

It is interesting to note, one author and researcher, who studied the resurrection from the basic assumption that it could not and therefore did not happen, changed his mind when confronted by the facts. Frank Morison (13), an English journalist, started to write a book proving the resurrection did not occur. To his credit, he at least maintained an open mind, as he went about researching and considering the facts. As he did, it became obvious to him that his original assumptions were wrong and he ended up writing a classic book on the resurrection. The reader is encouraged to read, "*Who Moved The Stone?*" if you have not already done so. It is an unusual person who, once having taken a strong position, as Morison did, will admit they were wrong and support the very opposite position based on the facts they encounter.

Regarding this book the author has taken the following positions as starting points for the play and dialog.

1. If Jesus was who he said he was, namely the Son of God, then for him to rise from the dead was possible, though it is not common to human experience.
2. The Bible is a reliable source of historical information regarding the events which occurred during the Passover weekend in 30AD.

Regarding the Bible, this is not the place to do an extensive defense of it as a reliable purveyor of truth; however, anyone wishing to pursue this avenue of thought is referred to McDowell's (11) *"Evidence That Demands A Verdict",* particularly chapter 4, where he presents persuasive evidence to support the validity of the Bible. It is interesting to note that those who argue against the resurrection, primarily Spong (17) and Schoenfield (15), still use Biblical references to develop their cases. Their problem is they use some facts and not others. They selectively use those that make their points and rule out those Biblical truths, which prove them wrong. This writer believes they are forced to do this because they start from the wrong assumptions and, therefore, will not accept any Biblical truths, which contradict them. Had they had more open minds, as did Morison, they to might have come out where we have, namely certifying JESUS OF NAZARETH AROSE.

Regarding Jesus himself, it is almost impossible to look at the facts and decide he was just an ordinary human being. What are the chances that an itinerant teacher from the non - descript town of Nazareth could, in about three years of teaching, so affect the world as Jesus has? All three major world religions accept Jesus, as a special and unique individual, even if not the Son of God. In the Koran (16), the holy book of Islam, Jesus is said to have been born of a virgin, to have done mighty works, including raising the dead, and to have been taken to heaven by God without suffering death. The Moslems accept most of his teachings, as well. Islam stops short of declaring Jesus was the Son of God, but they accept nearly everything else about Jesus Christians do. The Jews also accept Jesus as a great teacher and accept many of his teachings, but not those regarding his divinity. It is hard to see how a Jew can look at the Messianic prophesies from the Old Testament and not see that Jesus fulfilled all of them. Today many Jews are coming to see Jesus as the Christ, and they are accepting him as the Messiah in growing numbers.

Even atheists cannot deny the influence Jesus' brief ministry has had on the world. Western time is calculated from the time of his birth, millions of people have had life changing experiences based on his teaching, his teachings have had an immeasurable impact on organizations and governments worldwide, and the symbol of his death, the cross, can be found worldwide on buildings, in jewelry, and elsewhere. Could all of this have come from a man who did not know who he was and who lied about his nature, as well as his life death and resurrection? I think not. The facts cry out for a different interpretation than that. Namely, that he was who he said he was and that he did arise and defeat death, on our behalf, as he said he would!!

In this book the Bible is accepted as a true and valid purveyor of the historical facts regarding the events surrounding Jesus' death and resurrection. In the notes below, the scriptural references are presented as they are related to the incidents in the play. Also below you will find the authors explanation for why certain people and events are portrayed as they are. Could the events have happened as portrayed in the play? The answer is, yes! Did they happen exactly as presented here? Quite possibly they did. Certainly the major elements happened as portrayed. Some of the minor details may have been somewhat different, as noted below, and certainly the language and idiom were different, but it could have happened essentially as it is presented.

NOTES

Note 1 – The stipulation

The stipulation is reasonable, as a starting point in this play. No reasonable scholar any longer denies a person named Jesus of Nazareth lived in the first century. The oldest and most complete history of the period (9) mentions Jesus on at least three different occasions and mentions him with Pontius Pilate (9, P 379). Flavius Josephus was born a Jew named Joseph ben Matthias in 36AD. He became a Jewish rabbi and Pharisee. He later fought against the Romans. When the Jews lost, he went over to the Romans and became a Roman citizen assuming a Roman name, Flavius Josephus. At about 33 years of age he set out to write a history of the Jewish people. He wrote two major books one entitled "Antiquities of the Jews", and another "Wars of the Jews." Both are included in "The Complete Writings of Josephus" (9). Some scholars have contended Christians later added the passages regarding Jesus to authenticate him. In the appendix of the "Writings," the translator William Whiston, makes a powerful argument, as to why this was not so (9 P-637-647). Whiston also mentions some 26 ancient writers who accepted the writings of Josephus including the passages regarding Jesus. For anyone to believe today, that Jesus did not live in the first century is to deny the massive facts that he did. In addition, it should be added, that many of the historical characters involved in the play and story of Jesus are also mentioned in Josephus, and other histories of Rome, including Tiberius, Pontius Pilate, Caiaphas, Gamaliel, Annas, Herod, John the Baptist, and James the brother of Jesus. These facts reinforce the validity of the Biblical account.

If one wishes further information about the reality of the life of Christ the author strongly recommends the reading of the persuasive book by Dr. Gary Habermas entitled, "The Historical Jesus, Ancient Evidence of the Life of Christ" (7).

One of the most profound and prolific historians of the 20th century, Will Durant, has, with his wife Ariel, written 10 volumes on the history of civilization. Durant, who was an agnostic, entitled one of his volumes "Caesar and Christ" (Simon and Schuster, 1944) and on page 557 he says, "After two centuries of higher criticism the outlines of the life, character, and teaching of Christ, remain reasonably clear, and constitute the most fascinating feature in the history of Western man."

In summary it is fair to assume Jesus of Nazareth lived, was a remarkable person, was crucified under Pontius Pilate, was buried, and his body disappeared. It is historical fact the body was never found.

Note 2 – Andrew brings Peter to Jesus – John1: 35:51

Note 3 – Peter's view of Jesus, and conversation with Mary

It is highly probable that Peter had one or more conversations with Jesus' mother about him and the events Portrayed here - Luke 1:26-38, Matt. 1:18-25, Matt. 2:13-18, Luke 2:41-52.

Note 4 – Miracles of Jesus

Jesus is known as a miracle worker, even by those who are not Christians. There are references to this aspect of his life in the Koran (16) see Surah III (3:45-51) and in secular history (1).

Halley (8) lists the following miracles of Jesus from the Bible (PP-469-70):

Bodily Cures

1. Nobleman's son healed - John 4:46-54.
2. Infirm man healed in Jerusalem - John 5:1-9.
3. Peter's Mother-in-law - Matt. 8:14-17, Mark 1:29-31, Luke 4:38-39.
4. A leper - Matt. 8:2-4, Mark 1:40-45, Luke 5:12-15.
5. A paralytic - Matt. 9:2-8, Mark 2:3-12, Luke 5:17-26.
6. Man with withered hand - Matt. 12:9-14, Mark 3:1-6, Luke 6:6-11.
7. Centurion's servant - Matt. 8:5-13, Luke 7:1-10.
8. Two blind men - Matt. 9:27-31.
9. Deaf and dumb man - Mark 7:31-37.
10. Blind man at Bethsaida - Mark 8:22-26.
11. Blind man in Jerusalem - John 9.
12. Women of 18 years infirmity - Luke 13:10-17.
13. Man with dropsy - Luke 14:1-6.

14. Woman with hemorrhage - Matt. 9:20-22, Mark 5:25-34, Luke 8:43-48.
15. Ten lepers _ Luke 17:11-19.
16. Blind Bartimaeus - Matt. 20:29-34, Mark 10:46-52, Luke 18:35-43.
17. Malchus' ear - Luke 22:50-51.

Miracles over Nature

1. Water turned to wine - John 2:1-11.
2. Draught of fishes - Luke 5:1-11 (Near Capernaum).
3. Another draught of fishes - John 21:6.
4. Tempest stilled - Matt. 8:23-27, Mark 4:35-41, Luke 8:22-25.
5. 5000 fed - Matt. 14:13-21, Mark 6:34-44, Luke 9:11-17, John 6:1-14.
6. Jesus walks on the water - Matt. 14:22-33, Mark 6:45-52, John 6:19.
7. 4000 fed - Matt. 15:32-39, Mark 8:1-9.
8. Tax money - Matt. 17:24-27.
9. Fig tree withered - Matt. 21:18-22, Mark 11:12-14, 20-26.

Cures of Demoniacs

1. In the synagogue - Mark 1:21-26, Luke 4:31-37. (In Capernaum).
2. A blind and dumb demoniac - Matt. 12:22, Luke 11:14.
3. Gerrasene demoniacs - Matt. 8:28-34, Mark 5:1-20, Luke 8:26-39.
4. A dumb demoniac - Matt. 9:32-34.
5. The Syro-phoenician's daughter - Matt. 15:21-28, Mark 7:24-30.
6. The epileptic boy - Matt. 17:14-21, Mark 9:14-29, Luke 9:37-43.

Raising of the Dead

1. Jairus' daughter - Matt. 9:18-26, Mark 5:22-43, Luke 8:41-56.
2. Widow's son at Nain - Luke 7:11-15.
3. Lazarus at Bethany - John 11:1-44.

Beside the specific miracles listed above the Bible has summaries of many other miracles performed by Jesus. See John 2:23, Mark 6:53-56, Matt. 4:24, and John 21:25 for examples of these summaries.

Note 5 – Transfiguration of Jesus

Mark 9:2-8, Matt. 17:1-8, Luke 9:28-36.

Note 6 - Messianic prophecies and references

Mc Dowell (11) mentions there are over 300 Old Testament references to the coming Messiah, all of which fit Jesus. In Chapter 4 Mc Dowell catalogs 61 specific prophecies met by Jesus during his Life. These prophecies were written anywhere from 250 to 1500 years before the birth of Jesus and prove conclusively Jesus was the Messiah. (See next note).

Note 7 - Statistics on Messianic prophecy

The statistics were computed by Peter Stoner, a professor of statistics, and first appeared in the publication *Science Speaks*, Moody Press, 1963. The statistical calculations and format were reviewed and approved by a committee of the American Scientific Affiliation, an authoritative professional group of statisticians. Statistics is an honored scientific field widely used in scientific studies of many types. The calculations of Stoner, validated by other scientists, should speak volumes to those intellectuals who honestly seek facts and information about Jesus of Nazareth. This material is used with the permission of Moody Press.

Note 8 - Arrest of Jesus

Mark 14:43-52, Matt. 26:47-56, Luke 22:47-53, John 18:24.

Note 9 - Peter's Defense of Jesus

Mark 14:47, Matt. 26:51-53, Luke 22: 50-51, John 18:10-12. John reports that Peter was the one who drew his sword and cut off the ear of the servant of the High Priest. When Jesus healed the ear and told Peter to put up his sword, it is reasonable to assume the disciples became afraid. They knew Jesus had supernatural power and knew, if he used it, they could overcome the Temple Guard, however, when it became clear Jesus was not going to resist, they saw their vulnerability and ran away.

Note 10 - The Judas Kiss

It may be hard for us to understand why Caiaphas needed a person to identify Jesus for arrest. While Jesus was a popular person, it must be remembered there were no newspapers, TV, or pictures such as we have today. Also the arrest was being made at night and since men had beards and often had coverings over their heads it would have been very difficult for the guards to know which of a group of men was Jesus. Since the Temple Guard did not know Jesus, it was important they have someone who knew him well, so they would arrest the right person. This was even more important given the short time-frame available to arrest, convict, and execute Jesus before the Passover began.

Note 11 - Jesus' Trial
Mark 14:53, 55-65, Luke 22:54, 63-65, John 18:12-14, 18:24.

Note 12 - Darkness over the Land
Matt. 15:33-37, 27:45-50, Luke 23:44-46. An eclipse could have not caused the darkness over the land, as many might think, because an eclipse of the sun lasts at most 7-8 minutes. In addition scholars do not believe the moon was in the correct position for an eclipse at that time because Passover is held at the time of a full moon.

Note 13 - Other Phenomena
Mark 15:38-41, Matt. 27:51-56, Luke 23:45, 47- 49.

Note 14 - Peter and John to the Empty Tomb
Luke 24:9-12, John 20:2-10. Also see note 40.

Note 15 - Position of the Grave Clothes

The position and presence of the grave clothes (Luke 24:12 and John 20:7) is of significance. If someone were to have stolen the body of Jesus, it is not likely they would have taken time to unwrap the body, which would have been difficult, given how it had been prepared for burial. It would also have been time consuming and dangerous given the presence of the Roman Guard. On the other hand, the presence of the grave clothes and their position on the ledge, where the body had been, suggest the likelihood that Jesus exited them with little difficulty, without unwrapping them, even taking time to neatly fold the napkin, which had covered his head.

Note 16 - Roman Seal

The Roman seal, in the case of the tomb, was a cord placed across the stone in front of the tomb. The cord was affixed to the two sides of the tomb with sealing clay and the seal of the emperor was impressed into the clay, as it dried. This positioning of the cord and seal meant no one could move the stone or enter the tomb without breaking the seal and violating Roman law, which could mean a death penalty.

Note 17 - Appearance to Peter

Luke 24:34, I Corinthians 15:5. In this brief appearance to Peter on the first day Jesus might well have told Peter to get the disciples together that night, so he could appear to all of them at once.

Note 18 - Appearances of Jesus after Crucifixion

(from Halley (8) P- 526)

1. To Mary Magdalene (early morning) - Mark 16:9-10.
2. To the other women (early morning) - Matt. 28:9-10.
3. To two on road to Emmaus - Mark 16:12-13, Luke 24:13-32. (first day).
4. To Peter - Luke 24:34. (first day)
5. To the ten (Thomas absent) - Mark 16:14, Luke 24:36, John 20:19. (the night of the first day).
6. To the eleven (Thomas present) - John 20:26-31. (about a week later).
7. To the seven, beside the Sea of Galilee - John 21
8. To the eleven (and 500?) in Galilee - Matt. 28:16-20.
9. To James - I Corinthians 15:7.
10. Final appearance and ascension - Mark 16:19, Luke 24:44+, Acts 1:3+
11. Statements in Acts 1:3, 10:41, and 13:31 imply Jesus made numerous other appearances also during the 40 days prior to the ascension.

Paul reports a post-ascension appearance of Jesus to him in I Corinthians 15:5-8 and reinforces earlier pre-ascension appearances of Jesus including one to 500 followers at once.

Note 19 - Regarding the Questioning of Jesus' Followers

It is highly likely that the Bible would have reported it, if any of the disciples had been questioned or tortured to find out where the body of Jesus was. There is no evidence that any search or inquiry of any type was made. The Roman army freely tortured enemies to get information, in fact each legion had one or more specialists trained to do this

(6, P 230). In spite of the fact that a Roman seal had been broken, a capital offense, they did not arrest or question any follower of Jesus. Caiaphas had Peter and John arrested for preaching the resurrection, but he never questioned them about stealing the body. The quickest way for Caiaphas to resolve the matter would have been to produce the body of Jesus and prove he was not alive or arisen. The fact he never did this, or ever asked the Romans to do it, seems to imply he was confused by the events and perhaps not certain himself the body had been stolen.

Note 20 - Peter's Death

It is a matter of history that Nero persecuted the Christians, and killed many, blaming them for the burning of Rome (4, PP 20-1). Both Peter and Paul were in Rome during this period and are believed to have been executed by Nero. Peter would have been crucified as tradition suggests, but Paul would have been beheaded because he was a Roman citizen, and as such could not be crucified. Gibbons (4, P 8) describes historical recognition of the deaths of Peter and Paul in Rome only 150 years after their martyrdom.

Note 21 - Peter's Denial

Mark 14:54, 66-72, Matt. 26:58, 69-75, Luke 22:54-62, John 18:15-18, 25-27.

Note 22 - Sadducees and Pharisees

The differences between these two Jewish religious groups at the time of Jesus are significant. The Sadducees focused on obeying the written Jewish law or Torah. They denied there was a life after death and a resurrection of individuals to a new life. The Pharisees on the other hand believed in a life after death and a resurrection to a new life. (9, PP 376-7). The Pharisees also were looking for the coming of the Messiah. Caiaphas was a Sadducee and less likely to be sympathetic to Jesus' teaching about the law and life after death, than would be Pharisees like Joseph of Arimathea, Nicodemus, and Gamaliel. The Pharisees were more numerous and their beliefs prevailed to a greater degree than did those of the Sadducees in Jesus' time. The Sadducees died out as a religious group after the Romans destroyed the Temple in 70AD.

Note 23 - Did Jesus Try to Start a New Religion?

There is absolutely no evidence that Jesus tried to do this. He was the fulfillment of Jewish prophecy and sought to return to the faith of his fathers. Neither Jesus nor any of his disciples sought to set themselves up as, or to profit from becoming, a new religion. It wasn't until many years after the death of Jesus, that Christians began to see themselves as separate from the Jewish faith. In the early days of Christianity, the followers of Jesus were mostly Jews and continued to practice Jewish religious customs and practices. Paul and the apostles most frequently preached in the Jewish synagogues. Only later when the Jews were dispersed, the Temple at Jerusalem was destroyed (70AD), and the number of gentile Christians grew, did Christians begin to see themselves as separate from the Jewish faith.

Note 24 - Judas' Betrayal
Mark 14:43-52, Matt. 26:47-56, Luke 22:47-53, John 18:2-12.

Note 25 - Caiaphas asks Jesus if He was the Christ
Matt. 26:63-66. (Also see note 33).

Note 26 - Why Caiaphas Likely Contacted Pilate the Evening of Jesus' Arrest
Whether Caiaphas contacted Pilate the night before is not known for certain. There are reasons to believe he did. The author believes, as does Morison (13), that Caiaphas did contact Pilate. This would explain how Pilate's wife knew of Jesus and could explain why she dreamed about him that night and knew her husband would be dealing with him that Friday morning. It would also explain why Pilate had time available on a busy calendar to deal with Jesus. Pilate was headquartered in Caesarea and was only in Jerusalem for the Passover week. One can imagine how many people must have wanted to see him while he was there. It would be logical to assume Caiaphas, knowing of the impending arrest of Jesus, and the need for hasty action to crucify Jesus before the Sabbath and Passover week celebration began, would have made sure the night before that Pilate would be

available to affirm the Sanhedrin's verdict. Because of the Passover week celebration, if Jesus had not been crucified on that Friday, they would have had to wait a full week to crucify him. Caiaphas did not want Jesus in jail for a week because of his fear the followers of Jesus might disturb his plans for getting rid of Jesus. It is logical to assume Caiaphas did everything necessary to crucify Jesus, including contacting Pilate in advance to make sure he was available to affirm the verdict of the Sanhedrin.

Note 27 - Appearances before Pilate and Herod

Mark 15:1:15, Matt. 27:2, 11-26, Luke 23:1-25, John 18:28-19:16.

Note 28 - Barabbas and His Reason for Being in Prison

Barabbas had killed a legionnaire in the revolt in Jerusalem that developed over Pilate's use of the Corban (see Note 34). Pilate's use of Temple funds without permission of the High Priest or Sanhedrin led to an uprising in which Barabbas had been involved. He killed a legionnaire, and was convicted of murder.

Note 29 - Reason for Haste in Crucifying and Burying Jesus

Because the Jewish Sabbath started at sundown (6:00PM) on Friday and because it was against their law to execute anyone on the Sabbath (or in this case during the Passover week celebration), it was necessary to have the execution of Jesus complete (meaning he, and the two thieves crucified with him had to be dead and buried before 6:00PM). See also John 19:31.

Note 30 - Piercing of Jesus' Side
John 19:32-42.

Note 31 - Light and Angel at the Tomb
Matt. 28:2-4.

Note 32 - Caiaphas and Story of Jesus' Body Being Stolen
Matt. 28:11-15. Caiaphas as a Sadducee, who believed the spirit died with the body and that there was no life after death, must have believed there was a logical explanation for what had happened, yet he could not explain what had happened at the tomb. He got the soldiers to agree to a story, which he may have believed to be true, but which would have gotten the soldiers executed for sleeping on duty. Thus the bribe to the soldiers and promise to intercede with Pilate, if any questions were asked.

Note 33 - Illegality of the Trial and Conviction of Jesus
The trial of Jesus was illegal in several aspects. (3, p-77) It was against Jewish law to hold a trial at night, if the death penalty was involved. Jewish law also required at least two witnesses to agree regarding an offense before a person could be convicted. In fact, if they could not get two witnesses to agree, they were mandated to acquit the defen-

dant. In addition there was a requirement that a 24 hour period pass before a death sentence could be carried out. During that period the High Priest was required to fast before reaffirming the sentence and allowing the death penalty to be carried out. It was unusual, and some say illegal, for the judge (In this case Caiaphas, the High Priest) to question a defendant and for a defendant to be convicted based on his answer alone. Furthermore, to be convicted of blasphemy under Jewish Law a person had to invoke the name of God in their statement, something Jesus did not do. God's name was invoked by Caiaphas not Jesus. Suffice it to say, the arrest, trial, and execution of Jesus, as was done, was illegal in several aspects. It is interesting to note that in *The Archko*, Volume (12) there purports to be the translation of the minutes from a meeting of the Sanhedrin after Jesus' crucifixion, which was called to ask Caiaphas about irregularities in his handling of the trial of Jesus. History shows, that in 36AD, the same year Pilate was recalled to Rome, Caiaphas was removed as the High Priest in the Temple. This unjust conviction of Jesus fulfills the prophecy found in Isaiah 53:8.

Note 34 - Reasons Why Pilate was Sensitive to Caiaphas and Allowed Jesus to Die

It is historical fact that Pilate had serious trouble with the Jews not long before Jesus' crucifixion. (9, P-379). Pilate wanted to build an aqueduct into Jerusalem to enhance the city's water supply. He either did not have the money to pay for it or felt, since it was for Jerusalem, they should pay for it. Without permission Pilate took money from the Corban, which was a fund under control of the High Priest at the Temple. This led to a major problem for Pilate including an armed confrontation with some Jews, in which Barabbas killed a legionnaire. Caiaphas appealed the matter all the way to the emperor Tiberius in Rome. Tiberius backed the Jews and forced Pilate to back down embarrassing him and giving Caiaphas and the Jews some leverage over Pilate in the matter of Jesus. The delegation from the Sanhedrin, which went to Rome to meet with Tiberius was headed by Gamaliel, indicating the high esteem in which he was held by his colleagues.

It should be noted here that during this time Tiberius had at least 4 revolts going on in other parts of the empire (2, Tiberius) and probably wanted to avoid any others, if at all possible.

The incident of the Corban followed an earlier incident where Pilate attempted to place Roman symbols and a statue of the emperor in Jerusalem. Every major city occupied by Rome had such symbols to remind the people who their rulers were. The Jews seriously objected to the statue and ensigns on grounds that to accept them would be to violate the second commandment regarding graven images. Pilate persisted until the Jews threatened to revolt, if the images were not removed. When faced with this level of resistance Pilate backed down and removed the statue and symbols, objected to by the Jews.

It is interesting to note, that five years after the crucifixion of Jesus, Pilate had trouble with the Samaritans. They were gathering at their holy mountain (Mt. Gerizim) when Pilate came to believe they were plotting a revolt. He had his soldiers capture and kill some of the best young men in Samaria to try and dissuade them from a revolt. The Samaritans protested to Tiberius, which led to Pilate's recall, removal, and ultimate banishment from Rome into exiled. This is historical fact. (9, P-380).

The fact the Jews had successfully protested to Tiberius, and had backed Pilate down on another issue, made him sensitive to pressure on the matter of Jesus. Knowing these facts makes it easier to understand why Pilate would give into Caiaphas and permit the execution of an innocent man.

Note 35 - Lazarus, Mary, and Martha and Their Home in Bethany

Bethany is less than 2 miles from Jerusalem on the road to Jericho. This is the route Jesus and the disciples would have used to go to and from Galilee. It is likely that Jesus often stayed with them, when he was in the Jerusalem area, since their home was less than a half hours walk from the Temple area. It is clear Lazarus, Mary, and Martha were strong followers and supporters of Jesus. Jesus' raising of Lazarus from the dead and the subsequent action by Mary in anointing Jesus with expensive ointment in Bethany, just a few days before his crucifixion, further reinforces this point.

Note 36 - The Raising of Lazarus

John 11:1-44.

Note 37 - Thomas to Bethany

We are not told where the disciples, other than Peter and John, went when they fled during Jesus' arrest. It is very logical to assume that some or all went to Bethany. The reasons are several. First, the Garden of Gethesemane is to the east of Jerusalem, just off the road to Bethany, which is also east of Jerusalem. It is unlikely Thomas and the others would risk going back into the city. Second, they may have been staying in Bethany, which they often did when in the area, and Jerusalem was over flowing with people who had come for the Passover festivities. Thirdly, it is likely the disciples would have wanted to warn Lazarus and other followers in Bethany about the arrest of Jesus, because it put them all in potential danger. The priests had already consulted about killing Lazarus (See John 12:10). Lastly, if the disciples decided to get out of Jerusalem and head back to Galilee, they would have gone through Bethany.

For all these reasons it is logical to assume Thomas headed for Bethany after fleeing the arrest at Gethsemane. He likely went into hiding, since he was not with the other disciples, when Jesus made his first appearance to them, after his resurrection, on the first day of the week.

Note 38 - Mary of Bethany at Crucifixion and Resurrection

Following Mary of Bethany's anointing of Jesus in Bethany (see note 40) the Bible makes no further mention of Mary, her sister Martha, or her brother Lazarus. It is hard to believe, given their commitment to

Jesus and proximity to Jerusalem, they were not involved in the fateful events of that weekend. It is very likely Mary and Martha were there for the crucifixion with the other women followers of Jesus. The Bible does mention the women, both at the cross and at the tomb on Easter Sunday. Lazarus may well have been in hiding, possibly with Thomas and others, however, the women were not threats to the priests and Caiaphas, they likely joined the other women, mostly from Galilee, who had come to Jerusalem with Jesus and his mother for the Passover.

It should be noted here, the Bible often does not specify *everyone* who is present at an event. We are told there were women followers of Jesus at the crucifixion, and some are named, such as Mary of Magdalene and Jesus' mother but not all of them are mentioned. We are told in Matthew 15:40 that "among" the women at the burial were Mary Magdalene, Mary the mother of James and Jose, and Salome. The "among" strongly implies there were others. The same can be said about the women who came to the tomb on the first day of the week to anoint the body of Jesus. Could Mary of Bethany have been among these women? The answer is, yes. It is not only probable, but it is quiet likely. If Mary had not been at the crucifixion and tomb on Easter morning, would that change anything of consequence in the play or verdict? The answer quite simply is no! The words she speaks about the resurrection could have also been spoken by Mary Magdalene or one of the other women who were there. In short the writer believes there is good evidence Mary of Bethany was there, but if she wasn't, it makes no difference to the substance of the arguments and verdict.

Note 39 - The Burial of Jesus
Mark 15:42-46, Matt. 27:57-60, Luke 23:50-54, John 19:31-42.

Note 40 - Mary's Anointing of Jesus
Mark 14:3-9, Matt. 26:57-60, John 12:2-8.

Note 41 - Was Jesus' Tomb Known by his Followers?
Mark 15:47, Matt. 27:61-66, Luke 23:55-56. If one travels to Jerusalem today there are two different sites, which are held out as Jesus' burial sites. The site of the greatest credibility is in what is now the Church of the Holy Sepulcher. The other site is known as the Garden Tomb. Both possible burial sites are within a 100 yards or less of where Jesus was said to have been crucified. It makes eminent good sense to believe that Jesus' mother, John, and the other women, who were at the crucifixion, would have been concerned about where Jesus was going to be buried, so they could pay their respects and anoint the body after the Sabbath was over. They could literally see the tomb from the crucifixion hill and undoubtedly watched as Joseph prepared the body for burial. The idea some have put forth, that Jesus was buried in an unmarked paupers grave with the thieves (Spong 17), and no one knew where he was buried, is farfetched. Also hard to defend is the position of some, that the followers of Jesus went to the wrong

tomb on the first day of the week. John, Mary Magdalene, and the other women were at the crucifixion and visibly saw where the tomb was located. In addition, if they thought they might have gone to the wrong tomb, they certainly would have searched for the right one. There is no evidence they did. Instead we have an angel telling Mary Magdalene Jesus had arisen, followed closely by several appearances of Jesus to his followers. The arguments against the resurrection, which focus on the fact people did not know where Jesus was buried, are very weak at best.

Note 42 - Centurion's Servant Healed by Jesus
Matt. 8:5-13, Luke 7:1-10.

Note 43 - Did Caiaphas Contact Pilate the Night Before?
(See Note 26).

Note 44 - Pilate's Wife and her Dream about Jesus
Matt. 27:19.

Note 45 - The Offering of Barrabas
Mark 15:6-11, Matt. 27:17-21, Luke 23:18-19, John 18:39-41.

Note 46 - Pilate Washes his Hands
Matt: 24-26.

Note 47 - Pilate's Trouble with the Jews

It is a matter of record in secular history that Pilate had these problems with the Jews. His attempt to get the Jews to pay homage to the Roman symbols and his use of money from the Temple treasury (called the Corban) both got him in trouble and along with a later incident (see next note and note 34) finally got him recalled and exiled.

Note 48 - Pilate's Recall and Exile

It is a matter of Roman history that Pilate, a few years after the crucifixion of Jesus, had another confrontation with the Jews. (9, P-380). He thought the Samaritans were planning an uprising. As a preemptive move he took and executed some of their best young men. This caused a great uproar and another protest to Tiberius. Tiberius evidently had enough of Pilate's rash behavior and recalled him to Rome. Pilate was exiled for his treatment of the Jews and failure to effectively administer Palestine. Tradition says he committed suicide.

Note 49 - Eclipse of the Sun?

Astronomers are able to calculate the movement of the moon and stars, both forward and backward in time. The time assigned to Jesus' crucifixion was a time when there could not have been an eclipse of the sun, which produced the darkness. In addition, a full eclipse of the sun has never lasted more than 7-8 minutes, not 3 hours. This reinforces the position that the darkness indeed was a heavenly sign, which accompanied Jesus' crucifixion along with the other signs, namely the tearing of the Temple veil and reports of some opening of tombs with the dead appearing, for a time, to those who had known them. (Also see note 13).

Note 50 - Why Joseph of Arimathea Did Not Meet with the Sanhedrin

It is clear that the Sanhedrin had discussed Jesus' rising popularity before, especially after the rising of Lazarus and the driving of the moneychangers out of the Temple. It is also clear that some Pharisees had open minds about the teachings of Jesus, namely Nicodemus and Joseph. It is likely Caiaphas knew their feelings about Jesus and that they might have argued against any quick action to crucify him. This is why it is likely Caiaphas did not notify Nicodemus or Joseph of either the night trial or the early morning meeting to validate the late night trial, which was illegal. Luke 23:51 indicates that Joseph "did not consent to the council and deed" regarding the Sanhedrin's action regarding Jesus. This means he either was there and did not vote for the conviction or that he wasn't there. The latter position is taken in the play. Matthew 27:57 and John 19:38 both identify Joseph as a disciple of Jesus, though a secret one, as noted in the passage in John.

Note 51 - Caiaphas Called Before the Sanhedrin

The Archlo Volume (12) reports that Caiaphas was called before the Sanhedrin to report on his handling of the matters surrounding the crucifixion. (12, PP 97-116). This book also contains a report from Caiaphas to the Sanhedrin about the events at the tomb (12, PP 117-127). Therein Caiaphas reports talking to the soldiers who were at the tomb and each told the same story about what happened. The story they told was identical to the description of events given by Petronius in this book, namely the light, earthquake, being frozen, and seeing a man come out of the light to roll away the stone.

Note 52 - Joseph of Arimathea Asks for Jesus' Body

Mark 15:42-46, Matt. 27:57-60, Luke 23:50-54, John 19:38-42. It is reasonable to assume Joseph asked for the body of Jesus because of the respect he had for him. Had he not taken it, the body Jesus would have been buried with the two thieves in an unmarked grave in a potter's field.

Note 53 - Jewish Burial Procedures

Jewish burial procedures were quite different than those of the Egyptians, whose procedures are probably best known to Americans through the mummies we have seen in pictures or museums. The Egyptians, when preparing a body for burial would first remove the brain and all internal visceral organs (1). They would then fill these body cavities with balsamic herbs and other substances. They would then immerse the body in carbonate soda and fill the arteries and veins with balsams. Then they would complete filling the torso of the cadaver with bituminous and aromatic substances and salt (1). Lastly they would wind the body with cloths saturated with similar substances. The preparations were aimed at preserving the body, preventing decay and avoiding the odors of bodily decay.

In contrast the Jews did not remove any bodily organs nor inject any fluids into the body. They simply washed the body and the laid the body on the lower half of a linen sheet or shroud about 14' long and 4' wide. Next they folded the top half of the shroud down covering the whole body. They then placed a linen napkin over the head. The body was then wrapped with linen strips about 12" to 14" wide inside of which were placed spices and aloes (1). The spices and aloes combated the odor of decay and may have retarded the decaying process a bit. It was not unusual to use 70 to 100 pounds of spices and aloes to prepare an adult body for burial. The aloes were usually in the form of a paste so, that when applied within the strips of linen, it formed a sort of soft cast around the body.

The Jews would also bury their dead the same day they died, or the next day if a person died late in the day. Bodies were often buried in the many caves found in Israel or in burial places carved out of a hill, which was the case in Jesus' situation. It was common practice then for people to mourn for days during which time friends would come, mourn with the family (see the story of Lazarus for an example), and possibly visit the tomb and anoint the body with aromatic ointments, which showed their respect and also countered the odors of decay. Mary Magdalene was following this later custom with the other women, when they visited Jesus' tomb on the first day of the week, only to find he had arisen from the dead.

Note 54 - Nicodemus Visits Jesus by Night
John 3:1-21.

Note 55 - Gamaliel's Defense of Peter and John
Acts 5:34-40. This is powerful statement to the validity of Jesus' claim to be the Messiah, when we look back on history. Gamaliel the Elder, was one of the most respected Pharisees on the Sanhedrin and was elected as president of this 70 person High Court more than once. He was the grandson of the most respected rabbi Hillel. When he spoke others listened. He indicated there had recently been other men (Theudas and Judas of Galilee) who had claimed godly power, but when these leaders were slain their movements died out. He said, if Jesus was who he said he was, there was nothing they could do to stop him, and, if he wasn't, his movement would die as the others had. He also said, if Jesus was the Messiah, and they opposed him they would be striving against God. It is interesting that the leading Pharisee at the time had an open mind, as to who Jesus was, after the events of that Passover weekend. Gamaliel was right in what he said and history has proven Jesus was who he said he was, because no one, even the Roman Empire, was able to stamp out Christianity. No one remembers the other people Gamaliel mentioned, but Christianity has overcome

every persecution and has grown worldwide, as Gamaliel said it would, "If it is of God."

Note 56 - The story of Joseph of Arimathea

This story is very believable. The Bible says he was a Pharisee, which means he believed in the coming of the Messiah and in life after death. It is logical to assume that he was well aware of John the Baptist and John's comments regarding Jesus. Matthew 27:57 and John 19:38 indicate Joseph was a disciple of Jesus (though secretly, as John mentions). It is reasonable to believe an open minded religious teacher of the day would have found Jesus' teachings fascinating (as did Nicodemus, a friend). Even, if Joseph did not accept everything Jesus said, it is reasonable to assume, he believed Jesus had not been dealt with fairly by the High Priest and Sanhedrin. To help do what he could, he offered to help bury Jesus, offering his families tomb as a resting place. This act fulfilled a biblical prophecy found in Isaiah 53:9 where it says, "His grave was assigned to be with wicked men, yet with a rich man in   his death." In normal circumstances Jesus would have been buried in an unmarked grave in the potter's field, as were the two thieves crucified with him, yet because of Joseph of Arimathea he was buried instead in a rich man's tomb thus fulfilling another prophesy made hundreds of years before.

Christian tradition has it that Joseph of Arimathea not only became a Christian but that he carried Christianity into Europe and England, as a missionary before he died. It seems likely that he became a Christian after the events of that weekend in 30AD, but less likely that he became a missionary and went to Europe and England.

Note 57 - Names of the Centurions

Christian tradition has a centurion named Longinus at the crucifixion site. Whether this is true or not is not definitely known. Roman history does record the presence of a centurion named Cassius Longinus in the Middle East around this time in history (9, P-496) He is later listed as a legate in Syria. Walter Wangerin Jr. in his book "The Book Of God" (Zondervan 1996) also named the centurion at the cross Longinus (P-809). The case is similar for the other centurion Petronius. Such a centurion is recorded by Roman history as being in Jerusalem at the time of Jesus, (9, P-480) and he too later became a high Roman official in Syria. The names of these centurions are the only names of those called as witnesses, who do not appear in the Bible. As far as the play and story go, whether these are the actual names of the centurions involved or not makes no difference at all in the outcome.

Note 58 - The Roman Legion

There was a 12th Roman Legion and they were called the "Thunderbolts". This legion did serve in the middle-east and was recorded by Roman history as being there in 30AD. (6, p-293). They could have been in Jerusalem at the time of the crucifixion. The chances are they were the legion that crucified Jesus, however, whether it was the 12th, 13th, or one of the other legions of Rome makes no difference in the story. Interestingly the 12th Roman Legion suffered a severe defeat at the hands of the Jews about 37 years after the crucifixion (9, P-495-6). It is the only legion ever defeated by the Jews. The Roman legions in 30AD were organized, as stated in the play. Earlier legions had centuries with 100 men, which is where the names century and centurion come from, but they were gradually reorganized during this period and more often contained 80 men.

Note 59- Roman Crucifixion

Crucifixion was a cruel method of putting people to death. It was used from the 6th century B.C. until the 4th century A.D. (1). It was used by the Persians, Egyptians, Carthagins, and Romans. Rome used it only for slaves and criminals. It was forbidden by Roman law to crucify a Roman citizen. The crucifixion protocol required the prisoner be scourged (whipped) first, and then carry the cross (most often just the cross beam) from the point of scourging to the point of crucifixion. Crucifixion was abolished in the Roman Empire by Constantine I (who had become a Christian), out of respect for Jesus. It is interesting to note that Jesus' crucifixion actually led, some years later, to the abolition of this cruel form of death and undoubtedly saved many people from this inhumane experience.

The amount of time it took for a crucified person to die varied widely depending on many factors including their physical condition, how hard they were scourged, whether the nails pierced major arteries, whether they went into shock, the weather conditions etc. The period of time could vary from two or three hours to a day or more.

The Romans often left those they crucified on the crosses for days or weeks not only until they died, but until the vultures ate the bodies. The Romans thought allowing all to see those crucified would be a deterrent to others. The relatively short period Jesus and the thieves were on the cross was, as is stated in the play, because of the start of the Jewish Sabbath and Passover feast, which began at 6:00PM (sundown) on that Good Friday. Jewish religious practice did not allow the bodies to be on the cross during the Sabbath and Passover.

Note 60 - The Drugs and Wine

Crucifixion was one of the most horrible means of death. It is easy to understand that there were those who would do what they could to reduce the suffering. Women from the city would often offer those being crucified a drink of wine with a drug to dull the pain at the crucifixion site. Jesus was offered the drink but refused it. Mark 15:23, Matt. 27:23.

Note 61 - Jesus on the "Via dolorosa"

Mark 15:20-23, Matt.27:31-34, Luke 23:26-33.

Note 62 - Did Jesus Die on the Cross?

Modern medical authorities who read the resurrection story believe it has the "ring of truth" to it. The description of the piercing of the side of Jesus and the description of the flow of blood and water (lymphatic fluid) certainly conforms to what modern medical knowledge knows about what happens internally when a person dies. In addition to this we must believe the Romans could tell whether a person was alive or dead. They were experts at crucifixion, and the soldiers, who carried it out, had seen many dead and wounded people in their days as soldiers. The obvious visible signs of death were lack of breathing, fixed eyes which were unresponsive to light, no heart beat, no bleeding from obvious deep wounds, and after a time, rigor mortis. It is highly doubtful that a person could be living who showed the first four of these signs and certainly was dead when fifth appeared.

Note 63 - The Centurion's Conversion

Mark 15:39-40, Matt. 27:54, Luke 23:47. It is reasonable to assume, since they were in the same legion, that Longinus and Petronius knew each other and talked about the events of the crucifixion and resurrection and that all of this led to the conversion of Longinus.

Note 64 - Doubting Thomas

John 20:26-31. Someone has said Thomas doubted that others might believe. His response to the resurrection is very human and it has the "ring of truth" to it.

Note 65 - A Sorcerer Tries to Buy Christian Power

Acts 8:1-25. This is an interesting event, which indicates the power the apostles had after Pentecost, and which Jesus had in even greater measure before, was far greater than the power of the greatest sorcerer and magician of the day.

Note 66 - The Opening of the Tomb

Matt. 28:2-4. A stone large enough to cover an opening, through which people could pass, would be very large. It is unlikely it could be moved by one or two men, even very strong men. The fact the soldiers reported one person moved it, argues for a supernatural event.

Note 67 - The Positioning of the Guard

It is reasonable to assume the Romans positioned their men around the tomb basically as described here. They certainly would have had a perimeter guard. It is also significant that there is no evidence any Roman soldier was engaged or injured that night or that their perimeter guard was breached. This is strong evidence for a supernatural opening of the tomb.

Note 68 - Torture in the Roman Army

Each legion had one or more professionally trained torturers assigned to them (6, P 230). This was their method of obtaining information from prisoners in order to assist the legion in their mission. It would have been easy for the Romans to pick up one of the followers of Jesus (both Peter and John were in prison shortly after the crucifixion) and to torture the truth from them as to who stole Jesus' body and broke the Roman seal. The fact this did not happen, suggests they were not sure his body was actually stolen. The fact that the army was good at torture and getting information also suggests they probably knew which Jews were dangerous to them and possibly plotting revolt. It was obviously known to them that neither Jesus, nor any of his close followers, were plotting a revolt against Rome, as Caiaphas suggested. A group called the Zealots was interested in armed revolt against Rome during this period. There is no indication that Jesus' followers were Zealots. It is also likely the Romans knew who most of these Zealots and their leaders were.

Note 69 - No Questioning of the Disciples

If any of the disciples or followers of Jesus had been questioned or tortured to find out who took Jesus' body and where it could be found, there would have been mention of it in the biblical record. There is none, because it did not happen. We must then ask why did they not question the disciples or attempt to find the body? The answer must be that they were not at all sure it had been taken by Jesus' followers and that something had happened at the tomb they could not explain.

Note 70 - Who Guarded the Tomb?

There are differences of opinion regarding who guarded the tomb of Jesus. The confusion arises largely from the words of Pilate as recorded in Matt.27: 65 where, when asked by Caiaphas to make the tomb secure, Pilate responds "ye have a watch (guard)" and he tells them to go and make the tomb secure. These words of Pilate have been interpreted two ways. One sees them as saying to the High Priest you have your own guard (the Temple Guards) use them to make the tomb secure. Others read these words as saying, in effect, he granted them their request to have a Roman guard. The case for it being a Roman guard is stronger because a Temple guard would not have the authority to place a Roman seal on the tomb nor to enforce the Roman law making breaking the seal a serious violation of law meriting a death penalty. The Archko Volume (12) claims the guard was a part of the Royal City Guard and that a captain in that guard by the name of Malkus assigned responsibility for the assignment to a man named Ben Isham. That description agrees with that in the play regarding the number of soldiers assigned to guard the tomb. Whether it was Jews or Romans guarding the tomb makes little difference and has no bearing on events that occurred that fateful morning. The truth is the tomb was guarded by armed soldiers, the tomb was opened in a miraculous way, and Jesus did arise from the dead.

Note 71 - The Passover Plot

The basic position of The Passover Plot by Schonfied (15) is stated here, namely that Jesus' followers plotted to have him drugged, so he would not die on the cross, and then have Joseph of Arimathea retrieve the body and tend his wounds. This claim that Jesus never died leaves far more questions unanswered than answered. This position does not have many serious supporters.

Note 72 - Mary Magdalene's Healing

Mark 16:9. Mary Magdalene is sometimes confused with Mary of Bethany and the woman taken in adultery in John 8:3. She is, because of the latter confusion, sometimes called a prostitute. Susan Haskins has written an entire book on Mary Magdalene entitled "Mary Magdalene - Myth and Metaphor", Harcourt and Brace, Orlando, Florida, 1993. 818PP. In this highly researched book Haskins indicates there is no evidence she was a prostitute. In fact she was likely the daughter or widow of a wealth person, because she is mentioned as being one of the women who ministered to Jesus "out of their substance" (see Luke 8:2) indicating she had wealth. Her association with prostitution may come in part because the town of Magdala from which she came had a reputation for debauchery and was destroyed in 75AD. Mary became the first person charged by Jesus to spread the good news after His resurrection.

Note 73 - Mary Magdalene at the Tomb

John 20:11-18.

Note 74 - Appearance to the 500

I Corinthians 15:5-3. Also see statements in Acts 1:3, Acts 10:41, and Acts 13:31. These later verses imply Jesus appeared to many after the resurrection and did some additional teaching. It is logical to assume Mary Magdalene was at one or more of these appearances.

Note 75 - Mary Magdalene and John

Tradition has it that Mary Magdalene continued her work by supporting the apostle John, as she had Jesus. Tradition also has her being martyred for her faith in Ephesus.

Note 76 - Jewish - Christian Split

After Jesus' ascension his followers continued his teaching, but they also continued in their Jewish faith and practices. In addition Jerusalem became the center of their activity. The Christian faith was presented first to the Jews and later to the gentiles. It was only after the Romans destroyed the Temple in 70AD and scattered the Jewish nation that the Christian faith began to be perceived as a separate religion, no longer tied to the Jewish practices. The spread of the faith to the gentiles and throughout the Roman Empire along with the destruction of Jerusalem set the stage for Christianity to become a separate faith. At no time during Jesus' life or immediately thereafter did he or his followers seek to set up a new religion.

Note 77 - Moneychangers and Temple Tax

See Matt. 17:24-27. Once a year all Jews 20 years or older had to pay a tribute or Temple tax. This tax was started in the days of Nehemiah (See Neh.10:32) and was used to support the work of the Temple. In

Jesus' day the tax was 2 silver drachmas and was about the equivalent of pay for one days labor. The tax was paid in the month preceding Passover and had to be paid in the silver drachma minted in Tyre. No other currency was accepted because the Jews would not permit the Temple tax to be paid in a currency, which had a graven image on it. They felt to accept such a currency for the work of God in the Temple would violate the second commandment. This made it necessary to have moneychangers, who would change the common currencies of the day, principally the Roman money into drachmas so the Jews could pay the tax. These moneychangers would go out into the land of Israel during the month prior to Passover to change money and to collect the tax. Some were always in the Temple as well, but their numbers in the Temple swelled during the week of Passover to serve the multitudes that came to Jerusalem to celebrate this important feast. Some money-changers were dishonest and charged exorbitant sums to change the money.

Note 78 - Gamaliel and Saul of Tarsus (Paul)
Acts 22:3.

Note 79 - Gamaliel's Defense of Peter and John
Acts 5:33-40. This logical defense of Peter and John before the Sanhedrin by one of the most respected Pharisees of the day, is often over looked for its reason and meaning. Gamaliel in effect said, if Jesus' movement was of God, they could do nothing to stop it and, if it wasn't

of God it would die, as others had, when their leader died. Time and history have proven Jesus was of God, because nothing has been able to stamp out his truth. In spite of massive persecutions Christianity has survived stronger than ever, proving, by Gamaliel's logic, "it is of God".

Note 80 - The Koran and Jesus

It may surprise many Christians to know that Jesus and his teachings are held in great respect in Islam. The Koran, their holy book written by the prophet Mohammed, indicates Jesus was born of a virgin, did many miracles, including raising the dead, and was finally taken to heaven by God without dying, when his life was threatened by his enemies. Moslems will deny Jesus was the son of God, but do accept him as a very important prophet. Those interested should read Surah 3:45-51, and Surah 4:157-58 in the Koran.

Afterword

There are some products related to "The Resurrection – Ruse or Reality?" that readers may wish to consider using. They are as follows:

1. An abbreviated and modified form of the book has been developed into a play, which can be given in a theatre or church. The play has 8 witnesses rather than the 10 in the book and can be performed in a 2 hour period, which includes a 20 minute intermission. The play is titled, "The Resurrection on Trial."

2. Instructional materials have been developed for those who would like to use the book as a textbook for a 13- week course on the crucifixion and resurrection. Student study guides and a teacher's manual are available.

Anyone interested in these materials can write, or e-mail the author for further information on costs and how to obtain the materials to:

L. James Harvey
6732 Gracepoint Dr.
Caledonia, MI 49316

E-mail: theharveys77@yahoo.com
Web site: www.sentencesermons.com

Other Books by Dr. Harvey:

1. 701 Sentence Sermons
   (Grand Rapid, Michigan, Kregel Publications: 2000)

2. 701 More Sentence Sermons
   (Grand Rapids, Michigan: Kregel Publications, 2002)

3. 701 Sentence Sermons - Volume 3
   (Grand Rapids, Michigan: Kregel Publications, 2005)

4. 701 Sentence Sermons - Volume 4
   (Grand Rapids, Michigan: Kregel Publications, 2007)

5. Every Day Is Saturday (with Jackie Harvey)
   (St. Louis, Missouri: Concordia Publishing House, 2000)

6. Letters From Perverse University
   (Lincoln, Nebraska: Author's Choice Press, 2001)

7. Seven For Heaven (with Jackie Harvey)
   (Lima, Ohio: CSS Publishing Company, 2003

8. Does God Laugh?
   (Traverse City, Michigan: BMS Publications, 2008)

9. Run Thru the Tape
   (Rapid City, South Dakota: CrossLink Publishing, 2009

About the Author

Dr. L. James Harvey is a Christian author and speaker. He has authored 10 Christian books and currently writes a monthly column for the West Michigan Christian News entitled, "Encore Tidbits for Seniors."

Dr. Harvey has been a college professor, dean, vice-president, community college president, and a senior vice-president and partner in an international management consulting firm based in Washington D.C. He is an honors graduate of Hope College and has M.A. and Ph.D. degrees from Michigan State University. Dr. Harvey has had a lifelong interest in the facts surrounding the Resurrection of Jesus Christ, an event at the heart of the Christian faith.

Dr. Harvey currently lives in Caledonia, Michigan. He and his wife Jackie are members of Calvary Church in Grand Rapids, Michigan.

CPSIA information can be obtained
at www.ICGtesting.com
Printed in the USA
FFOW04n1925260215
11292FF